# PRESIDENTIAL VETOES
# AND PUBLIC POLICY

# STUDIES IN GOVERNMENT
# AND PUBLIC POLICY

# PRESIDENTIAL VETOES
# AND PUBLIC POLICY

RICHARD A. WATSON

UNIVERSITY PRESS OF KANSAS

Published by the University Press of Kansas (Lawrence, Kansas 66049),
which was organized by the Kansas Board of Regents and is operated
and funded by Emporia State University, Fort Hays State University,
Kansas State University, Pittsburg State University, the University of
Kansas, and Wichita State University

Permission to draw on previously published articles by the author has
been given by Sage Publications for "The President's Veto Power," *Annals* (September 1988), and the Center for the Study of the Presidency
for "Origins and Early Development of the Veto Power," *Presidential
Studies Quarterly* (Spring 1987). Material from "Veto Power" is ex-
cerpted with permission of G. K. Hall & Co., an imprint of Macmillan
Publishing Company, from *The Harry S. Truman Encyclopedia*, ed.
Richard S. Kirkendall (Boston: G. K. Hall/Macmillan, 1989).

Library of Congress Cataloging-in-Publication Data

Watson, Richard Abernathy, 1923–
    Presidential vetoes and public policy  /  Richard A. Watson.
    p.   cm.
    Includes index.
    ISBN 0-7006-0620-3
    1. Veto—United States—History—20th century.  2. Item veto—
United States.  3. Executive power—United States—History—20th
century.  4. Presidents—United States—History—20th century.
    5. United States—Politics and government—20th century.  I. Title.
JK586.W37   1993
320.4′04′0973—dc20                                                    93-15887

Printed in the United States of America
10 9 8 7 6 5 4 3 2 1

To Joan

# CONTENTS

# TABLES

# TABLES

# PREFACE

Woodrow Wilson, himself both a president and scholar, characterized the veto power as the president's "most formidable prerogative." Despite that fact, there have been only two books published on the subject in this century—one by Carlton Jackson in 1967 and a more recent one by Robert Spitzer published in 1988. Both of those books illuminate a number of features of the president's veto power, but they do not treat the subject as broadly nor did the authors utilize the diverse methodological approaches or sources that this study does.

Chapter 1 traces the origin of the veto back to Rome and discusses its use in England and the British Empire as well as states in this country. It also discusses the establishment of the presidential veto power in the United States and its evolution through the first century and a half of our existence. In addition, it analyzes legal issues relating to the president's veto power, including the unresolved one relating to the pocket veto. The chapter draws upon historical sources, both in this nation and abroad, and on court decisions relating to the veto.

The major part of the book, Chapters 2 through 5, focuses on presidential vetoes during the eight presidential administrations of Roosevelt through Carter. This political era, commencing with the "Roosevelt revolution" and ending with the rise of the "Reagan counterrevolution," covers nearly half a century during which time almost one-half of all presidential vetoes were cast.

Chapter 2 analyzes the incidence of vetoes cast from 1933 to 1981, the factors affecting the use of the power, and the types of legislation on which the veto has been exercised. It utilizes statistical approaches and data to test these matters.

Chapter 3 studies the evolution and results of the process whereby the executive branch advises the president on whether to veto legislation, as well as the development of the veto message. This chapter draws primarily on the materials contained in seven presidential libraries, the Library of Congress, the National Archives, the records of the Bureau of the Budget, the Office of Management and Budget, and the Legislative Reference Division. Personal interviews are also utilized in this chapter.

Chapter 4 discusses the nonexecutive sources of influence on presidential vetoes, including those of members of Congress, state and local officials, persons representing political parties and campaign organizations, interest group spokespersons, and members of the general public.

Chapter 5 analyzes the reasons given in veto messages for presidents' use of the power and the public-policy effects of presidential vetoes. It is based upon a content analysis of veto messages and uses the *Congressional Quarterly* to trace developments in the legislative process that follows the exercise of presidential vetoes.

Chapter 6 focuses on the proposal to grant the president the item veto power. It draws upon historical and legal sources, as well as other developments at the national and state levels. Finally, in Chapter 7 I summarize the major findings of the study and make some personal observations relating to the president's veto power.

# PREFACE

A study that is this broad in scope and that utilizes such a variety of approaches and sources could have been conducted only with the cooperation and assistance of a large number of persons and organizations at all stages of the ten-year project. While acknowledging their contributions, I also absolve them of any errors of fact or interpretation.

I am particularly indebted to my wife, Joan Lee Watson. She not only helped edit and typed the entire manuscript, but she also worked with me in searching out information on presidential vetoes in the voluminous collections of the presidential libraries.

I was also greatly assisted by the University of Missouri–Columbia, which granted me three separate leaves and provided me with Graduate Research Council grants to help to defray the considerable expenses of the project. Also assisting in that latter matter were grants from the Earhart Foundation and from Project '87, a joint venture of the American Historical and Political Science Associations, to both of which I am most grateful.

I also was greatly assisted by the Brookings Institution, which awarded me a Guest Scholarship that facilitated my conducting personal interviews with officials in Washington, D.C. Members of the Brookings staff, Stephen Hess, Tom Mann, James Reichley, and James Sundquist, provided wise counsel on a number of facets of the study as did Norman Ornstein of the American Enterprise Institute. Political scientist Larry Berman wrote a helpful piece titled "How Not to Be a Stranger in a Strange Land," designed to help political scientists like me acclimate themselves to presidential libraries, and historian Richard Kirkendall advised me on the best use of the resources of those libraries. Staff members at the Roosevelt, Truman, Eisenhower, Kennedy, Johnson, Ford, and Carter libraries also helped guide my wife and me through the intricacies of research in those depositories. The same was true of persons at the Library of Congress, the National Archives, and the Bureau of the Budget, the Office of Management and Budget, and the Legislative Service Division.

Other political scientists also helped me with the study. Wayne Francis and Karen McCurdy explained the mysteries of statistical analysis and the use of the computer, and George Edwards furnished me with data of his own on public opinion ratings of presidents. Stephen Wayne provided constructive comments on a paper I gave on the reasons presidents veto legislation at the 1987 meeting of the American Political Science Association in Chicago.

A number of students also assisted me in various ways. Jon and Peggy Hawley provided housing for me and my family during part of my stay at Brookings; Stephen Schweitzer wrote a helpful paper on sources of the president's veto power; and Eric Anderson, Rob Baker, Casey Coffee, Jerena Giffen, Linda Gladden, Ted MacDonald, and Karen Parsons worked on various facets of the major part of the book.

Two reviewers of the manuscript, Louis Fisher and an unnamed one, provided helpful comments, and Fisher also provided me with materials and leads that were of great assistance in improving the manuscript. I also appreciate the continued interest of Fred Woodward of the University Press of Kansas in my study of presidential vetoes. Alice Levine helped make this book better and more readable.

Some parts of the book have already appeared in the *Annals of the Academy of Political and Social Sciences*, the *Harry S. Truman Encyclopedia*, and the *Presidential Studies Quarterly*. I am grateful to the editors of those publications for permission to use materials from those articles.

# 1

# ORIGIN, ESTABLISHMENT, AND DEVELOPMENT OF THE PRESIDENT'S VETO POWER

*Veto:* The power or right vested in one branch of a government to cancel or postpone the decisions, enactments, etc., of another branch, esp., the right of a President, governor, or other chief executive to reject bills passed by the legislature. [*The Random House Dictionary of the English Language* (New York: Random House, 1967)]

Today, among all the elected leaders of the major democratic nations of the world, only the American president possesses the executive veto power and uses it in the process of policy-making.[1] However, the origins of the president's veto power go back to the Roman Empire where it was established five centuries before the birth of Christ. Later, the veto power developed as a practice in sixteenth-century England as part of its constitutional system and was subsequently transplanted to America during the colonial period. After independence, the veto power was vested in the governors of some of the American states, and ultimately, a similar power was granted to the American president by the delegates to the Constitutional Convention of 1787. This chapter first discusses the forms of the veto in those previous societies and then focuses on the deliberations of the Constitutional Convention and how the veto power was both shaped by and differed from previous experiences with the veto. The chapter concludes with an analysis of the development of the president's veto power, including legal issues relating to the scope and procedures of that power and the ways in which the courts have dealt with these issues.

## ORIGIN OF THE PRESIDENT'S VETO POWER

The word "veto" comes from the Latin term *vetare,* meaning to forbid or prohibit. Thus, veto means "I forbid" (or prohibit). The power first appeared in the constitution of the early Roman Republic established in 509 B.C. when the upper-class families, called "patricians," overthrew the monarchy.[2] The Republican Constitution substituted two patrician executive officials, known as consuls (or magistrates) and elected by the Assembly for one-year terms, in place of the deposed monarch and granted each of them the right of veto (or "intercessio") over the acts of the other. This arrangement was designed to curb the exercise of arbitrary authority that had occurred under the monarchy, but it also created a great potential for stalemate, because either official could prevent an action instituted by the other. To avoid a paralysis in the conduct of governmental affairs, therefore, each consul was allowed authority over the city on alternate months, and when both were away from Rome in battle, they took command on alternate days.[3] The consuls, however, could and did act together, for example, to convene the Senate or Assembly as evidenced by the number of laws that bore their joint names.[4]

Thus the early phases of the Roman Republic were

dominated by the patricians. Not only were the consuls from that social class, but so were members of the Senate (who enjoyed life tenure). Moreover, after consuls had served their one-year terms, they regularly entered the Senate. As a consequence, they tended to accept the advice of the body in which they would later serve as junior members.[5]

In time, the common people, known as "plebeians," extracted representation for themselves in the political institutions of the Roman Republic, primarily by withdrawing from the city and refusing to return until their demands were met but also by threatening not to serve in the army.[6] They were represented by the plebeian officers, called "tribunes," who were granted a veto power over actions of the consuls. Originally the veto was restricted and could only be used to protect plebeians from injustice and violence, but it was later extended to protect all plebeian interests,[7] including those that involved bringing a bill before the Assembly.[8] In addition, the veto extended to motions passed by the Senate, which were merely advisory to consuls whose actions, in turn, were subject to a veto by a tribune. If there were a veto, the Senate's motion was an expression of opinion only and was not legally binding on anyone.[9] The veto power exercised by the tribunes presented the same potential problem as that associated with the patrician consuls: the danger of bringing the machinery of state to a standstill, which introduced a constant element of anarchy into the Roman state.[10]

Thus the veto was initiated in the Roman Republic as a means of checking the arbitrary exercise of political power. Both types of vetoes (that of the patrician consuls against each other and that of the plebeian tribunes against the patrician consuls) involved executive officials. It remained for the English to develop the form of the veto enjoyed by the American president—the power of the chief executive to prevent the enactment of measures passed by a legislative body.

## The Veto in England

The executive veto developed in England as a result of the historic conflict between the monarchy and the national legislature. The conflict can be traced to the period when the Teutonic tribes conquered England and brought with them the institution of a national council, called the *Witenagemot,* which all freemen of the kingdom attended.[11] As the English extended their territory, the great majority of freemen could not attend the meetings of the council, and many of those who did were essentially "the king's men."[12] The Norman Conquest of 1066 strengthened the legislative power of the kings, who remained supreme over the Parliament well into the reign of Edward III (1327–1377). Even after legislation began to originate in Parliament toward the end of that monarch's reign, the king continued to influence the law by exercising three prerogatives: creating it through royal proclamations, suspending legislation, and granting dispensations that affected the operation of statutory law.[13]

In time, however, Parliament assumed the dominant role in the making of the laws. Initially it petitioned the king to make a law on a particular subject, but he retained the right to make one quite different from the one contained in the parliamentary petition.[14] Eventually, however, the House of Commons insisted on drawing up a petition in the precise form of an act of Parliament, and by the beginning of the sixteenth century, that custom had become a firm practice. The king's role in legislation became restricted to accepting the law passed by Parliament

4

or withholding his approval with the expression, *Le roi s'avisera* ("the king will think it over").[15] Thus the veto became the only means by which the king could affect the law, particularly after he also lost the powers of issuing royal proclamations, suspending legislation, and granting dispensations that affected the operation of statutory law.[16]

Over the years, English monarchs differed in the use of the veto. In 1597 Queen Elizabeth rejected more bills than she accepted, but shortly thereafter, in 1606, James I approved all the measures passed by Parliament that year, explaining that he did so "as a special token of grace and favor, being a matter unusual to pass all Acts without any exception."[17] The refusal of Charles I to approve several important measures passed by Parliament is considered to be one of the major causes of the Revolution of 1643;[18] after the Revolution of 1688, Parliament began to seriously question the use of the royal veto. In 1707 Queen Anne withheld her assent from a Scottish militia bill; that constituted the last time an English monarch ever vetoed a legislative act. It has been suggested that the absolute nature of the royal veto (it is not subject to being overridden by the Parliament) was the major reason it fell into disuse.[19] Walter Bagehot, a leading scholar of the British constitution, also claimed that English custom was such that a Queen "must sign her own death warrant if the two Houses unanimously send it up to her."[20]

Thus, as in Rome, the veto in England developed as a means of preventing an arbitrary exercise of political power by having one part of the government check and balance another part. The English legal scholar, Sir William Blackstone, likened it to the situation that Cicero described regarding the Roman tribunes: The king did not have "any power of doing wrong, but merely of preventing wrong from being done."[21] Unlike the Roman tribunes, however, the king in exercising the veto was not supposed to be acting to protect the interests of the common people. What was to be balanced in the English constitution was not one *social class* against another but rather one *branch* of government (the executive) against another (the legislature). Moreover, the royal veto in England represented the monarch's last vestige of a once great influence over the legislative process and ultimately even this last power fell into disuse.

## Vetoes Affecting the American Colonies

Although the veto power in England fell into disuse as far as domestic legislation was concerned, it was prominent in governing the American colonies. In fact, two separate vetoes were applied to the acts of colonial legislatures. Colonial governors representing the Crown in the new land possessed the first. The British monarch possessed the second.

Under British theory, the representatives of the colonists had no "inherent right" to make laws; the legislative powers of the colonial assemblies were granted to them by the king through the governor's commission.[22] In time, these assemblies were granted legislative powers, but most of the governors of the colonies possessed absolute veto power over the assemblies (the exceptions were Maryland, whose burgesses refused to recognize any gubernatorial veto power, and Rhode Island and Connecticut, in which governors were popularly elected for only a one-year term). Governors were expected to use the veto power to protect the interests of Great Britain; in some instances, they wielded it to protect themselves. In Pennsylvania, for example, governors used it to ensure the payment of their salaries; as Benjamin Franklin explained, "It became the regular practice to have orders in his [the governor's] favor on the treasury presented along with the bills to be signed, so that he might actually receive the former before he should sign the latter."[23]

In some instances, however, colonial governors gave in to the pressures of colonial assemblies and assented to laws that were contrary to the interests of the ruling nation. In such cases, however, the Crown had a second line of defense—a veto of its own. For the most part, decisions to allow or disallow laws passed by colonial assemblies were made by the Board of Trade rather than the monarch, but his was the official action.[24] Many colonial laws—nearly 400 over a period from 1696 to 1765[25]— were struck down, including those enacted to restrain the slave trade.[26] The colonial reaction to such royal vetoes is reflected in the statement of complaints against the king that appeared in the Declaration of Independence: "He has refused his Assent to Laws, the most wholesome and necessary for the public good."

Thus, the vetoes that affected the American colonies were somewhat different than those that existed in either the Roman Empire or England itself. There was no attempt to use the veto as a means of balancing the interests of opposing social classes as was done in Rome. Moreover, although both the gubernatorial and royal vetoes applied against actions taken by colonial legislatures, unlike the situation in England, the check was not so much that of one *branch* of government against another as that of one *level* of government (the colonial power) against another (the colonies). In any event, the colonists' experiences with the vetoes wielded by both the governor and the British monarch helped shape the role that vetoes would play in some of the new state governments of the former thirteen colonies.

7

CHAPTER ONE

*The Veto in Early State Constitutions*

Given the experience of the colonists with the vetoes cast by both the colonial governors and the British monarch, it is not surprising that most of the early state constitutions made no provision for an executive veto over the actions of the legislature, which was generally the favored branch of government.[27] There were, however, three exceptions to that tendency. South Carolina, Massachusetts, and New York all established constitutions during the Revolution that granted the veto power to the chief executive of the state.

In South Carolina, the veto power turned out to be short-lived. Its temporary constitution of 1776 gave the chief executive officer—known as the president and commander-in-chief—an absolute veto power over legislation. When Governor John Rutledge used that power to negate a new organic law designed to create a permanent state constitution, however, the reaction was so strong that he had to resign his executive post. His successor signed the law, creating the constitution of 1778, despite the fact that it made no provision at all for an executive veto.[28]

In Massachusetts, the process worked in reverse. The Massachusetts legislative body, the General Court, drafted a constitution in 1778 that made the governor the president of the Senate but provided him with no separate veto power over legislation.[29] However, the proposed constitution was rejected by vote of the towns. Among the objections registered by such towns was the fact that the proposed constitution failed to provide adequate checks and balances, including that of the executive upon the legislature.[30] Ultimately in 1780 a constitution was adopted that granted the governor a qualified veto, which he was to exercise by returning the legislative measure, together with his objections to it, to the house in which it originated. His veto was subject to being overridden by a two-thirds vote in both legislative chambers. The constitution granted him five days to consider the measure, and if it was not returned within that period, it automatically became law.[31]

The third state, New York, provided for an unusual type of veto in its constitution of 1777. Measures passed by the legislature were considered by the Council of Revision, consisting of the governor, the chancellor, and the judges of the state Supreme Court. This body had the power to review such measures and ultimately to veto them if a majority of its members felt that they were improper. If that occurred, the measure was to be returned, along with the council's objections to it, to the chamber in which it originated. Both chambers could override the veto by a two-thirds vote. The council had ten days to consider a measure; if it was not returned within that time, it became law unless in the meantime the legislature had adjourned, in which case the measure would return on the first day of the meeting of the legislature after the expiration of the ten days.[32] The measure was then subject to being overridden.

Thus, the veto was present in the constitutions of only two states, Massachusetts and New York, when the delegates to the national Constitutional Convention convened in Philadelphia in May 1787. These two states, in many respects, provided key models for the Founders to formulate a veto for the president of the United States.

## ESTABLISHMENT OF PRESIDENT'S VETO POWER

The delegates who gathered in Philadelphia agreed not only that there should be some sort of national execu-

tive (the Articles of Confederation provided for none) but
also that the executive should possess the power to veto
measures passed by the legislative body. A number of
arguments were made in support of such a prerogative,
the principal one being that the executive needed such a
power in order to protect itself against encroachment of
the Congress. James Madison also felt that the executive
veto would help to prevent "popular or factious injustice"[33]
(by which he meant rule by the capricious majority or by
selfish minorities); it would be "an additional check
against a pursuit of those unwise and unjust measures
which constituted so great a portion of our calamities."[34]
James Wilson expressed the sentiment that the president
would benefit from special advantages in policy-making,
stating that as the "man of the people," the president
would have the fullest information about the nation's situation, including access to foreign and domestic records
and communications, as well as advice from executive
officers in the different departments of the general
government.[35]

But although the delegates were in agreement on the
desirability of an executive veto, they disagreed on the
form the veto should take. One basic issue was whether
the executive should exercise the veto in conjunction with
members of the judiciary (as was provided for in the New
York Constitution) or alone (as was done under the Massachusetts Constitution). Those favoring the joint exercise
said the judiciary alone would not be able to defend itself
against legislative encroachments;[36] moreover, permit-
ting the judiciary to share the veto power with the president would make the veto less objectionable than if the
president exercised it alone.[37] Madison also argued that
the president would be more firm in his resolve to use the
veto if he exercised it jointly with the judges. Finally, he

contended that having such judges share in the veto power would help to avoid the passage of laws that were "unwise in their principle or incorrect in their form."[38]

An equally wide range of arguments was arrayed against joining the executive and judiciary. Elbridge Gerry of Massachusetts contended that "the Executive while standing alone would be more impartial than when he could be covered by the sanction and seduced by the sophistry of the Judges."[39] He also feared that blending the judicial and executive departments in that way would "bind them together in an offensive and defensive alliance against the Legislature, and render the latter unwilling to enter into a contest with them."[40] Nathaniel Gorham of Massachusetts argued that "judges ought to carry into the exposition of the law no prepossessions with regard to them"[41] and that would not be the case if they were to participate in the exercise of the veto power. Luther Martin of Maryland argued that judges cannot be presumed to have a higher degree of "a knowledge of mankind" than legislators do and so should have no role in negating laws unless they are unconstitutional, in which case the laws would ultimately come before the judges anyway.[42] He also pointed out that judges "should have the confidence of the people" and feared that "this [confidence] will soon be lost, if they are employed in the task of remonstrating against popular measures of the Legislature."[43]

The issue was joined at the Convention when Charles Pinckney of South Carolina proposed that the veto be exercised by the president alone, and Edmund Randolph of Virginia countered with the suggestion that the chief executive share the veto power with "a convenient number of the national judiciary," the combined body to be known as the Council of Revision.[44] (This was the same designation that was used in the New York Constitution.) Initially the Randolph resolution became the basis on which the delegates proceeded with the matter, but eventually they adopted the Pinckney proposal in which the president exercised the veto alone. Thus, the Massachusetts form of this aspect of the veto prevailed over the New York one.

Another major issue with respect to the veto was whether it should be *absolute* or whether it should be *qualified*, that is, subject to being overridden by the two houses of Congress. Alexander Hamilton and James Wilson, advocates of a strong executive, favored an absolute veto. Aware that a veto in that form was suggestive of the royal veto under the British system, Wilson argued that an absolute veto would seldom be used and that its "silent operation would therefore preserve harmony and prevent mischief."[45] However, both the Pinckney and Randolph resolutions provided for the qualified veto, and that was the form adopted by the Convention.

A subsidiary issue also arose at the Convention regarding the qualified veto: What size vote should be required to override the president's veto? The Pinckney resolution set the figure at two-thirds of the members of each house, but Hamilton proposed that the requirement be raised to three-fourths on the grounds that a two-thirds requirement in New York State had been ineffectual in curbing laws passed by factions of its legislature.[46] Pinckney, however, argued that the three-fourths figure would be "putting a dangerous power in the hands of a few Senators headed by the president,"[47] and his position prevailed.

Another major decision regarding the president's veto power had to do with the number of days the president had to consider a law passed by Congress. At one point, a proposal was made that the period be one of seven days (which appeared to be a compromise between the Massachusetts practice of five days and New York's of ten days),[48] but ultimately the delegates adopted the ten-day figure. Eventually, the Convention departed from both state constitutions by providing that if the president did not act within the ten-day period and Congress had adjourned in the meantime, he was considered to have exercised a "pocket veto." Unlike a regular veto, the pocket veto was absolute because Congress could take no further action on the matter.

One other decision regarding the veto power should be noted: The delegates decided that it should only apply to national legislation. As Moe suggests, they did give serious consideration to what he terms a "national veto," whereby the central government (usually construed to mean Congress), like the British Board of Trade, would have reviewed all state acts and had the power to negate those that it felt conflicted with national laws or national interests.[49] However, he concludes that they ultimately decided to rely on the judiciary to enforce national supremacy over the states.[50] Spitzer also indicates that a proposal was floated to grant the president rather than the Congress the right to veto state laws but it did not receive much support or serious attention.[51]

Thus, the veto power that emerged from the deliberations of the Constitutional Convention became a potentially powerful weapon for the president in struggles with Congress. It remained to be seen, however, how that weapon would actually be utilized by chief executives.

## THE DEVELOPMENT OF THE PRESIDENT'S VETO POWER

More than three years passed in Washington's first administration before he made use of the veto power. On April 5, 1792, in a terse, three-paragraph veto message,

Washington negated a congressional apportionment bill. Almost five years passed before he cast his second and final veto on February 28, 1797, of a bill relating to the military establishment of the United States.

The two succeeding chief executives, John Adams and Thomas Jefferson, cast no vetoes at all, nor did Adam's son, John Quincy Adams, and James Monroe vetoed only one piece of legislation. The only early president to exercise the veto power with any frequency was James Madison, who vetoed 7 bills in all. Thus, the first six presidential administrations, covering a period of 40 years (1789–1829), witnessed a total of only 10 vetoes and, as indicated, 7 of these were attributable to Madison alone.

When early presidents did veto legislation, they tended to emphasize constitutional objections. Washington's first veto of the congressional apportionment bill was based on his contention that it violated constitutional requirements that representatives should be apportioned among the several states according to their respective numbers and that the number of representatives should not exceed 1 for every 30,000 inhabitants.[52] Madison's first 2 vetoes of bills relating to Protestant churches cited the First Amendment language: "Congress shall make no law respecting an establishment of religion."[53] His seventh and final veto of a bill providing funds for internal improvements was based on his contention that such an activity exceeded Congress's enumerated and implied powers.[54]

Early chief executives were generally reluctant to substitute their judgments on public-policy matters for those of the Congress. Washington explained his position in a letter to Edmund Pendleton: "You do me no more than justice when you suppose, that, from motives of respect to the legislature (and I might add from my interpretation of the constitution), I gave my signature to many bills, with which my judgment is at variance." He did so because he believed that the rejection of a bill "can only be justified upon the clear and obvious ground of propriety; and I never had such confidence in my own faculty of judging, as to be ever tenacious of the opinions I may have imbibed in doubtful cases."[55] Jefferson agreed that the chief executive should sign a bill "unless the President's mind on a view of everything which is urged for and against a bill is tolerably clear that it is unauthorized by the Constitution; if the pro and con hang so even as to balance his judgment, a just respect for the wisdom of the legislature would naturally decide the balance in favor of their opinion."[56]

Although constitutional objections to legislation were the major concern of early presidents, on occasion they did veto measures on other grounds. Washington's second veto of a congressional bill (relating to the military establishment) was cast because he considered it unwise.[57] In vetoing a bill regarding a national bank, Madison waived the question of its constitutionality (saying it had repeatedly been recognized as valid) and based his objections on the fact that it would not accomplish the financial purposes for which it was to be established.[58]

It was when Jackson assumed the presidency that the use of the executive veto power changed radically. He vetoed 12 bills in his eight years in office, more than all his predecessors combined. Jackson did not hesitate to substitute his judgment on policy matters for that of the Congress. At the same time, he also believed that he had the right to interpret the Constitution, a right that he would exercise not only against the contrary opinions of the Congress but against those of the Supreme Court as well. In his famous bank veto message (July 10, 1832), he cited constitutional grounds for his disapproval but also emphasized concerns of social and economic justice for the "humble members of society" to support his action.[59] One close student of the subject, Kallenbach, suggests that the veto message "was a powerful appeal to the citizenry of the country for their support, a masterful campaign document for the forthcoming presidential election."[60]

Subsequent presidents continued to differ on the proper reasons for casting a veto. Several who held office prior to the Civil War continued the early tradition. Van Buren pocket vetoed one bill, and William Henry Harrison, Taylor, and Fillmore vetoed no legislation at all. Even Lincoln, a strong chief executive, cast only 2 regular vetoes. His philosophy on the matter paralleled that of Washington: "As a rule I think the Congress should originate as well as perfect its measures without external bias."[61]

For the most part, however, what Kallenbach terms Jackson's "tribunative" view of the veto authority, ultimately prevailed.[62] Tyler used the veto on 10 occasions, which led his opponents in Congress to introduce a resolution to impeach him for "the high crime and misdemeanor of withholding his assent to laws indispensable to the just operations of government, which involved no constitutional difficulty on his part."[63] (The resolution failed.) Tyler's successor, James Polk, while vetoing only 3 bills, nonetheless subscribed to the Jacksonian view of the proper reasons for the president's use of the veto; in his Fourth Annual Message to the Congress, Polk stated: "But if at any time Congress shall, after apparently full deliberation, resolve on measures which he deems subversive of the Constitution or of the vital interests of the country, it is his solemn duty to stand in the breach and resist them."[64]

For the most part, early presidents who cast vetoes prevailed in their conflicts with Congress. This was even true of Jackson who frequently did battle with national legislators: Not one of his 12 vetoes was overturned by Congress. It was not until 1845, more than half a century after Washington cast the first presidential veto in 1792, that Congress successfully overrode an executive veto. In that instance, Congress overturned President Tyler's veto of a bill that prohibited the building of revenue vessels or steam cutters by order of the executive unless appropriations for such construction had previously been passed by Congress. Tyler's arguments that the public interest would be damaged by the bill and that it would violate contracts previously entered into for the construction of such vessels were unpersuasive as both houses overwhelmingly voted to override the veto on March 3, 1845, the day President Tyler left office.[65] Only one other pre–Civil War president, Pierce, suffered a similar fate: Of his 9 vetoes, 5 were overridden by Congress.

## Post–Civil War Developments

Important developments with respect to presidential vetoes continued in the period following the Civil War. Andrew Johnson, who succeeded to the office after the assassination of Lincoln, cast 29 vetoes, more than twice the previous high of 12 issued by Jackson. Moreover, 15 of his 21 regular vetoes that were subject to being overridden by Congress were overturned, three times the number overridden during the administration of Pierce. These battles between Johnson and Congress reflected basic differences between the two over the reconstruction program. Corwin attributes the difficulties to the fact that the president "took his constitutional beliefs with fearful seriousness" and defended them "as if they had been transmitted to him from Sinai."[66]

Johnson's successor, Grant, also wielded the veto power vigorously, setting a new record of 93. However, many of his vetoes involved private pensions and relief bills rather than major public legislation. Grant also was the first president to utilize the pocket veto extensively, in his case on 48 occasions (as compared to his 45 regular vetoes). Unlike the situation with Johnson, only 44 of Grant's 93 vetoes were overridden, which reflected the fact that the pocket vetoes were not subject to being overturned and that Congress was not disposed to even try to override regular vetoes of private pensions and relief bills.

The trends begun under President Grant reached new heights in the first term of Cleveland, who vetoed 414 bills, which as Spitzer notes, represented twice as many vetoes as all his predecessors combined.[67] Of these 414 vetoes, 343 (nearly 83 percent) involved private pension and relief bills.[68] Fisher suggests that Cleveland's position on what he regarded as pension abuses may have cost him the 1888 election (which he lost to Benjamin Harrison), as veterans campaigned vigorously against him.[69] However, Cleveland was reelected in 1892 and continued his veto practices, casting 170 vetoes in his second term, many of them involving private pension claims. As with Grant, many of Cleveland's vetoes were pocket ones, and only 7 of the 584 vetoes he cast in his two terms were overridden by Congress. The same pattern prevailed in the administration of Theodore Roosevelt: He vetoed 82 bills, many of them involving private pension bills and the use of the pocket veto; only 1 was overridden by Congress.

With the advent of the Taft presidency, the development of the veto changed. It was used on fewer occasions, but instead of relating primarily to private legislation, particularly individual military pensions and relief, it involved presidential conflicts with Congress over important issues of public policy. Taft vetoed legislation pertaining to tariffs, internal improvements, and immigration, and a proposal to allow voters in the new state of Arizona to recall judges. Wilson's vetoes also included immigration legislation as well as measures relating to World War I and its aftermath. The three conservative Republican presidents of the 1920s (Harding, Coolidge, and Hoover) vetoed legislation on such basic matters as bonuses for veterans (not individually but as a group), agricultural and general relief, and attempts to create a public corporation to provide inexpensive electrical power. All presidents cast their vetoes on the basis of fundamental philosophical differences with the Congress.

A comparison of the presidential vetoes during the 68-year period from 1865 to 1933 with those of the pre–Civil War period, constituting 76 years, shows some marked differences. During the latter period, there were a total of 1,075 vetoes and 44 overrides compared with 59 vetoes and 6 overrides of the former period. Moreover, as Spitzer points out, whereas the pre–Civil War period was characterized by considerable debate over whether a president could legitimately veto a bill that did not involve constitutional objections, in the latter period it was generally conceded that the president could negate any legislation he considered inappropriate for whatever reason. As he summarizes the situation in the latter period: "Presidential judgment continued to be questioned, but not the power that gave rise to the judgment." [70]

### Legal Issues Relating to the Scope and Procedures of the Veto Power

Although the language contained in Article 1, section 7, paragraphs 2 and 3, of the Constitution is fairly explicit with regard to the president's veto, a number of legal issues have arisen over the years regarding the scope of that power and the procedures relating to its exercise. In most instances, such issues have been resolved by actions of the parties involved, that is, the president and the Congress, but in some instances, it has been necessary to turn to the courts to settle such matters.

One issue involves the kinds of measures to which the veto applies. Article 1, Section 7, paragraph 2, states: "Every bill which shall have passed the House of the Representatives and the Senate shall, before it becomes a law, be presented to the President of the United States"; paragraph 3 of that same section uses broader language: "Every order, resolution or vote to which the concurrence of the Senate and the House of Representatives may be necessary (except on a question of adjournment) shall be presented to the President of the United States." Despite the broad wording, however, it has been determined by usage that the veto applies to regular bills and "joint resolutions" dealing with legislative matters of an unusual nature; however, "concurrent resolutions" relating to matters of organization, procedure, and opinion of concern only to both houses of Congress (as well as House resolutions and Senate resolutions that are of concern to just one chamber) are not subject to the president's veto.[71] Moreover, the Supreme Court ruled very early in *Hollingsworth v. Virginia*[72] that congressional actions relating to amendments to the Constitution did not have to be submitted to the president for his signature.

Other issues relating to the scope of the president's veto power have been resolved by presidents themselves. The view held by some members of Congress that the veto power covered only public and not private bills (those involving individuals or specific organizations) was first successfully challenged by President Madison (who vetoed the incorporation of a Protestant Episcopal church in Alexandria) and subsequently by a number of his successors.[73] Congressional assertions that presidential vetoes do not apply to matters relating to the "power of the purse" (because that is the oldest power vested in legislative bodies) met a similar fate: Madison vetoed expenditures authorized for internal improvements; Hayes, a general appropriation measure; and Tyler, revenue bills relating to tariffs.[74]

Procedural matters relating to the president's veto power have also been resolved both by usage and as a result of judicial decisions. Some of them pertain to the effect of congressional recesses and adjournments on presidential approvals of bills. It was determined in *La Abra Silver Mining Company v. United States*[75] that the president has the authority to approve a bill within the ten-day period following its presentation to him, even though the Congress was in recess on the day his approval was given to the measure. Subsequently, that approval authority was extended in *Edwards v. United States*[76] to the situation in which the Congress had adjourned sine die by the time a bill had been signed by the president.

The most controversial issue, however, with respect to the pocket veto involves the situation in which the president does *not* approve the bill within the ten-day constitutional period and Congress has, in the meantime, adjourned or recessed. In a 1929 ruling, *The Pocket Veto Case*,[77] a bill had been presented to President Coolidge less than ten days before Congress adjourned at the end of its first session; the Supreme Court held that the adjournment "prevented" the president from vetoing the bill and hence the pocket veto was valid. The Court also interpreted the "ten days" to mean calendar, not legislative, days.

Subsequently, the federal courts have ruled on other types of situations involved in congressional adjournments and recesses. In *Wright v. United States*,[78] the Senate recessed for a three-day period during which time the secretary of the Senate was able to receive a vetoed bill and in fact did so. The Court ruled that this arrangement did not prevent the return of the bill and to allow a pocket veto to apply in that situation would mean that the objections of the president would operate practically as an absolute veto, although Congress was ready to consider his objections.

Similar reasoning led lower federal courts to invalidate 2 pocket vetoes cast by President Nixon. The first one, challenged by Senator Edward Kennedy, occurred during a six-day intrasession adjournment of both houses of Congress during the Christmas season in 1970. A federal district court ruled in *Kennedy v. Sampson*[79] that arrangements made for the receipt of presidential messages during the adjournment allowed the bill to be returned to the Congress as part of the regular veto process; hence the pocket veto was without legal force. An appellate federal court subsequently affirmed the ruling and the Nixon administration did not take the case to the Supreme Court.[80] During a 29-day adjournment following the end of the first session of Congress in 1973, President Nixon again pocket vetoed a bill, and Senator Kennedy once again challenged its validity in *Kennedy v. Jones*.[81] The Justice Department consented to entry of judgment in favor of Senator Kennedy, as determined by President Ford. The Ford administration subsequently stated that it would use the regular veto rather than the pocket veto during intrasession and intersession recesses and adjournments of Congress, provided that the chamber to which the bill was to be returned authorized an officer or other agent to receive return vetoes during that period.

President Carter later honored the Ford accommodation with the Congress.

The accommodation with the Congress reached during the Ford and Carter administrations did not continue during Reagan's term. After Congress adjourned at the end of the first session of the 97th Congress, the president pocket vetoed a special bankruptcy reorganization bill. At the end of the first session of the 98th Congress when it was in a nine-week adjournment, the president vetoed a bill to require him to certify human rights practices in El Salvador as a precondition for military aid. A bipartisan group of members of the House of Representatives brought suit to require that the bill be published as a public law. However, the federal district court in *Barnes v. Carmen*[82] upheld the pocket veto; in so doing, it followed the precedent of *The Pocket Veto Case* involving adjournment at the end of a session and distinguished the current situation from the intrasession adjournment involved in *Kennedy v. Sampson.*

The case was appealed to the U.S. Circuit Court of Appeals and the ruling of the lower court was reversed.[83] The majority of the appeals court held that the members of Congress had standing to sue; that it had the duty to decide issues between Congress and the executive branch; and that the only adjournment that allowed the president to use a pocket rather than a regular veto was one at the end of a Congress, provided that Congress appointed agents to receive veto messages. In so ruling the court declined to distinguish between intrasession and intersession vetoes. Justice Robert Bork dissented on the basis that the courts should not become an umpire in disputes between the president and Congress and therefore that the members of the House of Representatives had no standing to sue.

The circuit court ruling was then appealed to the

Supreme Court. However, the majority of the Court held that the case was "moot" because the law had expired prior to its hearing the matter.[84] In so ruling, the Court said it made no difference that the case was not "moot" at the time the U.S. Circuit Court of Appeals heard it. Justice John Paul Stevens dissented, arguing that as long as the question whether the bill ever became a law continues to have practical significance, Congress retains its interest "in ensuring that its enactments are given their proper legal effect."[85]

Since the judiciary did not settle the pocket veto issue, Congress decided to move on its own in the matter. In 1989 Congressman Butler Derrick, Democrat of South Carolina, introduced legislation that was referred jointly to the House Rules and House Judiciary committees. Both issued reports in 1990[86] providing that pocket vetoes could only be used at the end of a Congress and that the clerk of the House of Representatives and the secretary of the Senate are authorized to receive bills returned by the president at any time their respective houses are not in session. However, House Minority Leader Robert Michel, Republican of Illinois, opposed the bill on the grounds that it would lead to a useless confrontation with the president, and Congressman Carlos Moorhead, Republican from California, argued that it would likely lead to a presidential veto and what was needed was not a new law but "a final, definitive ruling from the Supreme Court."[87]

Meanwhile the Democrats in Congress and Republicans in the executive branch are far apart on the issue of the pocket veto. The former contends that it only applies at the end of an entire Congress. The latter, as represented by the Reagan and Bush administrations, argues that the pocket veto may be used any time Congress adjourns for more than three days, a period it borrows from the language in Article 1, Section 5, that requires either House to obtain the consent of the other if it recesses for more than three days.[88]

Two other procedural matters relating to the president's veto power have also been resolved. It has been determined by usage that the ten-day period for presidential consideration of an enrolled bill does not begin to run until it is officially presented to him. Thus, presiding officers of the two houses can withhold their signature from passed bills in order to give the chief executive time to properly consider them.[89] The Supreme Court also ultimately settled in *Missouri Pac. Ry. Co. v. Kansas*[90] the issue regarding the meaning of a "two-thirds" vote of the two houses necessary to override a presidential veto by ruling that the extra-majority figure applies to a quorum of the two bodies (and not to their entire memberships). The practice of Congress has been to require a two-thirds vote of the members present and voting.[91]

With the historical and legal background of the president's veto power in mind, I now turn to the major part of this book: the functioning of that power during the modern political era on which this study focuses.

NOTES

1. As indicated subsequently, the monarch of Great Britain still theoretically possesses the power to withhold assent from measures passed by Parliament, but no British monarch has actually utilized that power since 1707.

2. Carl Roebuck, *The World of Ancient Times* (New York: Charles Scribner's Sons, 1966), pp. 437ff.

3. Ibid., p. 439.

4. H. F. Jolowicz and Barry Nicholas, *Historical Introduction to the Study of Roman Law*, 3d. ed. (Cambridge: Cambridge University Press, 1972), p. 47.

25

CHAPTER ONE

5. Roebuck, *World of Ancient Times,* p. 439.
6. Ibid., p. 440.
7. W. A. Hunter, *A Systematic and Historical Exposition of Roman Law* (London: William Maxwell and Son, 1885), p. 14.
8. Jolowicz and Nicholas, *Historical Introduction,* p. 12.
9. Ibid., pp. 44f.
10. Ibid., p. 14; see also Roebuck, *World of Ancient Times,* p. 442.
11. Edward Mason, *The Veto Power* (Boston: Ginn and Company, 1891), p. 12.
12. Ibid.
13. Ibid., p. 13.
14. William Edward Hearn, *The Government of England: Its Structure and Development* (London: Longmans, Green and Company, 1886), p. 57.
15. M. M. Knappen, *Constitutional and Legal History of England* (Hamden, Conn.: Archon Books, 1964), p. 257.
16. Mason, *Veto Power,* pp. 14f.
17. Hearn, *Government of England,* p. 60.
18. Mason, *Veto Power,* p. 16.
19. George Curtis, *History of the Origin, Formation, and Adoption of the Constitution of the United States* (New York: Harper and Brothers, 1858), 2:266.
20. Walter Bagehot, *The English Constitution and Other Political Essays* (New York: D. Appleton and Company, 1877), p. 125.
21. William Blackstone, *Commentaries on the Laws of England* (Boston: I. Thomas and E. T. Andrews, 1799), 2:156.
22. Leonard Labaree, *Royal Government in America: A Study of the British Colonial System Before 1783* (New Haven: Yale University Press, 1930), p. 218.
23. Jonathan Elliot, *The Debates in the Several State Conventions on the Adoption of the Federal Constitution* (Philadelphia: J. B. Lippincott Company, 1901), 4:621.
24. Oliver Dickerson, *American Colonial Government, 1696–1765* (Cleveland: Arthur H. Clark Company, 1912), p. 227. The author also notes (p. 226) that unlike a regular veto that prevents a proposed law from going into effect, the royal disapproval applied to laws already in force and thus had the effect of a legislative repeal.
25. Ibid., p. 227.

26. George Bancroft, *History of the United States from the Discovery of the Continent* (New York: D. Appleton and Company, 1883), 2:77.

27. The same situation prevailed at the national level under the Articles of Confederation, which provided for no executive branch at all.

28. Joseph Kallenbach, *The American Chief Executive: The Presidency and the Governorship* (New York: Harper and Row, 1966), p. 24.

29. Robert Taylor (ed.), *Massachusetts, Colony to Commonwealth: Documents on the Formation of Its Constitution, 1775–1780* (Chapel Hill: North Carolina Press, 1961), p. 56.

30. For example, the delegates to the Essex County Convention expressed that objection. Ibid., pp. 79, 87.

31. Ibid., pp. 131f.

32. Benjamin Perley Poore, *The Federal and State Constitutions, Colonial Charters, and Other Organic Laws of the United States* (Washington, D.C.: Government Printing Office, 1780), Part II, pp. 1332f.

33. Max Farrand (ed.), *The Records of the Federal Convention of 1787* (New Haven: Yale University Press, 1966), 2:587.

34. Ibid., p. 74.

35. Elliot, *Debates in the Several State Conventions*, 2:448. This argument was made before the Pennsylvania Convention called to ratify the Constitution.

36. Farrand, *Records of the Federal Convention*, 1:138.

37. Ibid., 1:99.

38. Ibid., 1:139.

39. Ibid.

40. Ibid., 2:78.

41. Ibid., 2:79.

42. Ibid., 2:76.

43. Ibid., 2:77.

44. Ibid., 4:622.

45. Ibid., 1:100.

46. Ibid., 2:585.

47. Ibid., 2:586.

48. Kallenbach, *American Chief Executive*, p. 61, n. 44.

49. Ronald C. Moe, "The Founders and Their Experience with the Executive Veto," *Presidential Studies Quarterly* 17,

no. 2 (Spring 1987): 423. As the author points out, however, this veto would have prevented laws from taking effect rather than disallowing those already in force.

50. Ibid., p. 424, citing Charles F. Hobson, "The Negative in State Laws: James Madison and the Crisis of Republican Government," *William and Mary Quarterly* 36 (April 1979): 228.

51. Robert J. Spitzer, *The Presidential Veto: Touchstone of the American Presidency* (Albany: State University of New York Press, 1988), p. 15, citing Farrand, *Records of the Federal Convention,* 3:399.

52. James D. Richardson, *A Compilation of the Messages and Papers of the Presidents, 1789–1897* (Washington, D.C.: Authority of Congress, 1900), 1:124.

53. Ibid., 1:489f.

54. Ibid., 1:584f.

55. Jared Sparks, *Writings of George Washington* (Boston: Russel, Shattuck and Williams and Hilliard, Gray, and Company, 1836), 10:371f.

56. Paul Leicester Ford (ed.), *The Writings of Thomas Jefferson* (New York: G. P. Putnam's Sons, 1895), 5:289.

57. Richardson, *Compilation of Messages,* 1:211f. (February 28, 1797).

58. Ibid., 1:555 (January 30, 1815).

59. Ibid., 2:590.

60. Kallenbach, *American Chief Executive,* p. 354.

61. Ibid., pp. 354f., n. 13, citing John C. Nicolay and John Hay, *Complete Works of Abraham Lincoln* (New York: F. D. Tandy Company, 1905), 1:697.

62. Ibid., p. 354.

63. *Congressional Globe,* 27th Cong., 3d sess., 1843, 12, p. 144.

64. Richardson, *Compilation of Messages,* 4:662 (December 5, 1848).

65. For a discussion of this historic override, see Carlton Jackson, *Presidential Vetoes, 1792–1945* (Athens: University of Georgia Press, 1967), pp. 83f.

66. Edward S. Corwin, *The President: Office and Powers, 1789–1948,* 3d ed. (New York: New York University Press, 1948), p. 28.

67. Spitzer, *Presidential Veto,* p. 61.

68. Jackson, *Presidential Vetoes*, p. 149.
69. Louis Fisher, *President and Congress: Power and Policy* (New York: Free Press, 1972), p. 97.
70. Spitzer, *Presidential Veto*, p. 59.
71. Kallenbach, *American Chief Executive*, p. 348.
72. 3 Dallas 378 (1798).
73. See Clarence A. Berdahl, "The President's Veto of Private Bills," *Political Science Quarterly* 52 (December 1937): 505–531.
74. Kallenbach, *American Chief Executive*, p. 349.
75. 175 U.S. 423 (1899).
76. 286 U.S. 482 (1932).
77. 279 U.S. 655 (1929).
78. 302 U.S. 583 (1938).
79. 364 F. Supp. 1075 (D.C.C. 1973).
80. Kennedy v. Sampson, 511 F. 2d 430 (D.C. Cir. 1974).
81. Civil Action No. 74-194 (D.D.C.).
82. 582 F. Supp. 163 (D.D.C. 1984).
83. Barnes v. Kline, 759 F. 2d 21 (D.C. Cir. 1985).
84. Burke v. Barnes, 479 U.S. 361 (1987).
85. Ibid., 366.
86. H. Rept. 101-417 (pt 1), 101st Cong., 2d sess., 1990; H. Rept. 101-417 (pt 2), 101st Cong., 2d sess., 1990.
87. *Congressional Quarterly Almanac* (Washington, D.C.: Congressional Quarterly, Inc., 1990), 46:22.
88. H.R. 849, *Hearings before the Subcommittee on the Legislative Process of the House Committee on Rules*, 101st Cong., 1st sess., 58, 1989.
89. This procedure was used when President Wilson was attending the Paris Peace Conference; bills were not presented to him until he returned to the United States. A similar procedure was validated by a federal court in 1964 when a bill was presented to President Eisenhower after a trip to Europe. Louis Fisher, *Constitutional Conflicts Between Congress and the President*, 3d ed., rev. (Lawrence: University Press of Kansas), pp. 122f, citing Eber Bros. Wine & Liquor Corporation v. United States 337 F. 2d 624 (Ct. Cl. 1964).
90. 248 U.S. 276 (1919).
91. Fisher, *Constitutional Conflicts*, pp. 121ff.

# 2

## PRESIDENTIAL VETOES FROM ROOSEVELT THROUGH CARTER: AN OVERVIEW

In this chapter, I present an analysis of presidential vetoes cast in the modern era, beginning with the administration of Franklin D. Roosevelt in 1933 and ending with that of Jimmy Carter in 1981. The first section focuses on the incidence of presidential vetoes cast from 1933 to 1981, with particular attention to the relative frequency with which the eight chief executives who served during this period utilized the veto power. The second part explores various factors associated with the incidence of vetoes cast during that period. The chapter concludes with an analysis of the kinds of legislation that recent presidents have vetoed.

### INCIDENCE OF PRESIDENTIAL VETOES

Table 2.1 shows the total number of vetoes cast by each of the presidents who served during this period. Franklin Roosevelt in just over twelve years cast 635 vetoes, even exceeding the 584 that Grover Cleveland exercised in his eight years in office. Next in line were Harry Truman and Dwight Eisenhower, whose 250 and 181 vetoes, respectively, rank them as third and fourth

CHAPTER TWO

TABLE 2.1. Vetoes Cast by Presidents Roosevelt through Carter, 1933–1981

| President | Bills Vetoed Private | Public | Total | No of Years Served | Vetoes Per Year |
|---|---|---|---|---|---|
| Roosevelt | 497 | 138 | 635 | 12.37 | 51.33 |
| Truman | 169 | 81 | 250 | 7.63 | 32.77 |
| Eisenhower | 103 | 78 | 181 | 8.00 | 22.62 |
| Kennedy | 12 | 9 | 21 | 2.90 | 7.24 |
| Johnson | 16 | 14 | 30 | 5.10 | 5.88 |
| Nixon | 3 | 40 | 43 | 5.69 | 7.56 |
| Ford | 5 | 61 | 66 | 2.31 | 28.57 |
| Carter | 2 | 29 | 31 | 4.00 | 7.75 |
| Total | 807 | 450 | 1,257 | 48.00 | 26.19 (avg.) |

SOURCES: *Presidential Vetoes, 1789–1976,* comp. Senate Library (Washington, D.C.: Government Printing Office, 1978); *Presidential Vetoes, 1977–1984,* comp. Senate Library (Washington, D.C.: Government Printing Office, 1985).

among all who have served in the office. In contrast, John Kennedy and Lyndon Johnson cast only 21 and 30 vetoes, respectively; of the presidents serving in this century, only Warren Harding with 6 vetoes exercised the power on fewer occasions.

In assessing the importance of vetoes cast by presidents, however, it is important to distinguish between those relating to private and public legislation. The former names a particular individual or few individuals or entity or entities (such as a business or few businesses) that is or are to receive relief from the federal government in the form of a claim based on a financial loss, the payment of a pension, a granting of citizenship, and the like. In contrast, a public bill relates to matters affecting all individuals and businesses or those belonging to certain categories or classifications. Thus, public bills are more significant because they affect a much broader range of individuals and groups than private bills do.[1]

Over the years Congress has provided means for trying to prevent spending too much of its time on bills that affect only one or a few persons or entities. One such means was the establishment of a Court of Claims to which such bills could be referred for consideration and recommendation as to their merits. Another was the enactment of laws authorizing executive agencies to act on cases previously handled by Congress.[2]

The Court of Claims was originally established in 1855. However, this court did not relieve Congress from the necessity of ultimately deciding on the merits of private bills. In his first inaugural message to Congress on December 3, 1861, President Lincoln requested that the court be given the authority to make final decisions on private bills. Lincoln stated, "The investigation and adjudication of claims in their nature belong to the Judicial Department . . . reserving the right of appeal on questions of law."[3] Congress did expand the powers of the Court of Claims in 1883 and again in 1887 but not to the extent Lincoln recommended.[4]

The procedure of referring private bills to the Court of Claims for recommendations to the Congress continued over the years. However, in a 1962 case, *Glidden Co. v. Zdanok*,[5] the Supreme Court ruled that the Court of Claims may only decide "cases and controversies" and may not render advisory opinions that other branches of the government are free to disregard. After that decision the Court of Claims declined to accept any other congressionally referred cases. As a means of meeting that objection Congress passed legislation in 1966 that provides for such cases to be referred to trial commissioners rather than to the Court of Claims itself.[6]

In the post–World War II period Congress took other

33

actions designed to relieve itself of the burden of dealing with private bills. In 1946 it enacted the Federal Tort Claims Act (Title IV of the Legislative Reorganization Act), which provided for settlement by executive departments and agencies of certain tort claims not to exceed $1,000 caused by negligent or wrongful acts of any employee of the U.S. government while acting under the authority of his or her office or employment. Similar claims exceeding $1,000 were to be settled by U.S. district courts. In 1966 the Congress eliminated the $1,000 maximum for agency-settled tort claims but added a provision that any award, compromise, or settlement in excess of $25,000 be affected only with the prior consent of the attorney general of the United States or his designee. The 1946 Legislative Reorganization Act also covered private claims relating to bridges and the correction of military records by review boards composed of civilians. In 1957 and 1958 Congress enacted laws that authorized the attorney general to deal with certain types of immigration appeals.

All of this legislation had the desired effect. Congress passed fewer private bills with which presidents had to deal. For example, in just over the five years of the Johnson administration, Congress passed 1,088 private bills; in the five and three-quarters years that President Nixon served, 496 such bills were enacted, and during the four years of the Carter administration, 293 private bills were passed. In addition, Presidents Nixon and Carter vetoed a smaller percentage (less than 1 percent of private bills that were passed by Congress) than any of the other six presidents. (For example, President Roosevelt vetoed about 1 in 8 private bills passed by Congress while Harry Truman negated about 1 in 20 such bills.) It should be noted from Table 2.1 that beginning with the Nixon administration vetoes of public bills far exceeded those of private ones.

Because of the declining importance of vetoes of private bills and also because the main focus of this study is on public policy-making, I decided to analyze only vetoes of public bills. However, not all public legislation is of equal importance. For example, some of it deals with essentially local matters, such as the sale of the Port of Newark army supply base to the City of Newark, or minor national legislation, such as the authorization of the postmaster general to operate motor vehicles seized for violations of custom laws. An analysis of the 450 public bills determined that 259 of them involved significant policies of concern to the nation.[7]

Table 2.2 focuses on the incidence of vetoes of public bills from 1933 to 1981, with particular attention to those

TABLE 2.2. Vetoes of Public Bills Cast by Presidents Roosevelt through Carter, 1933–1981

| President | All Public Bills | | No of Years Served | Signif. Bills Vetoed Per Year |
|---|---|---|---|---|
| | Non Signif. | Signif. | | |
| Roosevelt | 78 | 60 | 12.37 | 4.85 |
| Truman | 44 | 37 | 7.63 | 4.85 |
| Eisenhower | 44 | 34 | 8.00 | 4.25 |
| Kennedy | 5 | 4 | 2.90 | 1.38 |
| Johnson | 5 | 9 | 5.10 | 1.76 |
| Nixon | 2 | 38 | 5.69 | 6.68 |
| Ford | 6 | 55 | 2.31 | 23.81 |
| Carter | 7 | 22 | 4.00 | 5.50 |
| Total | 191 | 259 | 48.00 | 5.40 (avg.) |

SOURCES: *Presidential Vetoes, 1789–1976,* comp. Senate Library (Washington, D.C.: Government Printing Office, 1978); *Presidential Vetoes, 1977–1984,* comp. Senate Library (Washington, D.C.: Government Printing Office, 1985).

relating to legislation of national significance. The three most recent presidents analyzed in this study not only vetoed more public than private bills, as previously noted, but a large number of the public bills they vetoed were also of national significance. When the length of term is taken into account, all three of them cast more significant vetoes per year than did any of their five predecessors. The table also shows that President Ford's record of vetoes was the most important of the 1933–1981 period and those of Presidents Kennedy and Johnson were the least important.

Further distinctions can be drawn, however, as to the relative importance of legislation that has significance for national policy-making. In other words, some legislation is more vital to the nation's interest than other legislation. The problem is how to distinguish between those categories. Two criteria were utilized in attempting to make that distinction. One was whether the vetoed legislation was designated by *Congressional Quarterly Almanac* as involving a "key vote." The other was whether the vetoed legislation had been the subject of a roll-call vote when it was passed in either the House or Senate or in both chambers. For both criteria, the analysis includes only legislation on which the president exercised a regular veto.[8]

Since 1945, when *Congressional Quarterly* began publication, its editors have made judgments as to which legislative issues considered during each congressional session are "key" ones. In making that determination, they judge each issue in relation to one or more of the following criteria: (1) it is a matter of major controversy; (2) it is a matter of presidential or political power; (3) it has potentially great impact on the nation and lives of Americans. For each group of related votes on an issue, one key vote is usually chosen, which in the opinion of *Congressional Quarterly* editors was most important in determining the issue's outcome.[9]

Although the key votes are determined by members of the media who cover the activities of Congress, the roll-calls depend on the views of the members of Congress themselves. Article I, Section 5, of the Constitution provides that "the Yeas and Nays of the Members of either House on any question shall, at the Desire of one fifth of those Present, be entered on the Journal." Members of Congress typically request a roll-call vote on issues that are important and controversial and on which they desire their colleagues to take a public position.[10] Therefore, I examined the *Congressional Record* to determine whether legislation on which the president exercised a regular veto was passed in one or both houses by a roll-call vote.

Table 2.3 contains data on the relative importance of legislation vetoed by recent presidents, taking into account both the key votes and roll-call votes. It shows that Eisenhower's vetoes involved the greatest percentage of key vote legislation. From the standpoint of roll-call votes, however, Nixon's vetoes were the most important.

One final aspect of presidential vetoes cast during the 1933-1981 period should be assessed: Which of the eight presidents vetoed the most *historic bills* (those that have been highly controversial and/or of long-term importance to the nation)? This judgment is admittedly a very subjective one, but I believe that Harry Truman earns that distinction. Among the bills he vetoed were a number relating to both the domestic economy and internal security. In the former category were the Taft-Hartley bill, which proposed regulation of labor-management relations, and two bills that sought to convey title to offshore oil re-

CHAPTER TWO

TABLE 2.3. Relative Importance of Regular Vetoes of Nationally
Significant Legislation Cast by Presidents Roosevelt through
Carter, 1933–1981

| President | No. of Regular Vetoes | Key Votes No. | Key Votes Percentage | Roll-Call Votes No. | Roll-Call Votes Percentage |
|---|---|---|---|---|---|
| Roosevelt[a] | 38 | | | 11 | 28.95 |
| Truman | 30 | 12 | 40.00 | 18 | 60.00 |
| Eisenhower | 20 | 13 | 65.00 | 15 | 75.00 |
| Kennedy | 0 | 0 | 0.00 | 0 | 0.00 |
| Johnson | 4 | 0 | 0.00 | 1 | 25.00 |
| Nixon | 24 | 12 | 50.00 | 23 | 95.83 |
| Ford | 42 | 12 | 28.57 | 34 | 80.95 |
| Carter | 11 | 5 | 45.45 | 8 | 72.73 |
| Total | 169 | 54 | 41.22[b] | 110 | 65.09 |

[a]Since *Congressional Quarterly* did not begin publication until 1945,
there is no key vote information for the Roosevelt administration.
[b]This figure is computed on the basis of the 131 regular vetoes cast by
Presidents Truman through Carter.

sources (mistakenly referred to as "tidelands" oil) owned
by the national government to the states. In the other
category were the Internal Security bill sponsored by
Democratic Senator Pat McCarran of Nevada, which
would require the registration of communist and other
suspect groups with the attorney general and authorized
the detention of persons thought likely to commit es-
pionage and sedition, and the McCarran-Walter Immigration bill (named for McCarran and its joint sponsor,
Democratic Representative Francis Walter of Pennsylvania), which would control the immigration and deportation of "subversives" and persons with communist
affiliations. In addition to these historic pieces of legislation, President Truman also vetoed the Kerr bill (named
for Democratic Senator Robert Kerr of Oklahoma), which

would exempt independent gas producers from regulation by the Federal Power Commission, and three tax bills (presidents generally defer to Congress on revenue measures). Truman's own later assessment that he "found it necessary to veto more major bills than any other president with the possible exception of Grover Cleveland"[11] would also apply to the veto record of the six presidents I have analyzed who succeeded him in office.[12]

## FACTORS ASSOCIATED WITH VETOES

I now turn to another basic matter with respect to vetoes cast by Presidents Roosevelt through Carter: What were the major factors associated with the use of the veto power by those eight presidents? In order to analyze which factors most affected presidential vetoes cast between 1933 and 1981, it was necessary to devise a method for measuring the incidence of vetoes during that time span. I decided to use the criterium referred to in Table 2.2: the number of vetoes of public legislation of national significance cast during that period. That distinction has the advantage of focusing on the vetoes that have most relevance for national policy-making, a major focus of this study. It also parallels the approach used in statistical analyses of presidential vetoes by Lee, Copeland, Rohde and Simon, Hoff, and Woolley.[13] I used the calendar year as the unit of analysis.[14] Thus, the dependent variable in this study is the number of vetoes of public legislation of national significance cast each year.[15]

I divided the independent factors, or variables, into four major categories. The first has to do with the *personal backgrounds of the presidents* who served in the period from 1933 to 1981. The second includes matters relating to *presidential-congressional relations.* The third category pertains to the *presidents' standing with the American public.* The final category includes variables relating to the general *nature of the times* during the period under analysis.

## Personal Backgrounds of the Presidents

One personal background factor, or variable, that might affect presidents' inclination to use the veto power is their party affiliation. V. O. Key, Jr., observed in the 1960s that Democratic presidents have tended to subscribe to the principle that the chief executive should provide forceful legislative leadership whereas Republican presidents have generally leaned toward a more restricted view of their legislative role.[16] If this is indeed the case and if this observation holds for the more recent period as well, then one would expect Democratic presidents to have vetoed more bills during the 1933–1981 period than did their Republican counterparts. However, it is also possible to assume that because over the years Republican presidents have tended to be more politically conservative, they might have used the veto power more often than Democratic chief executives in order to prevent liberal legislation—typically calling for increased federal regulations and for expenditures—from being enacted into law.

Another potentially important background variable affecting vetoes is the kind of public office presidents held prior to becoming chief executive. One might expect, on the one hand, that those who previously served as governors (who also possess the veto power) might be used to exercising that prerogative and carry that inclination over into their experience as president. On the other hand, presidents who previously served in Congress might be more likely to defer to the role and expertise of national legislators in law-making and therefore be less likely to use the veto power. It is also possible that Congress itself might be more sympathetic to an ex-colleague and therefore be less inclined to send such a president a bill that he would be forced to veto. Fortunately, with the exception of Eisenhower, who was neither a governor nor a national legislator, all the remaining seven individuals who occupied the presidency during the 1933–1981 period previously served in one, but not both, of those official capacities (governor or member of Congress).

Table 2.4 indicates that in the period from 1933 to 1981 Republican presidents cast an average of about 8 vetoes a year, almost twice that of the Democratic chief executives. A great deal of that disparity is due to the exceptionally high veto record of President Ford. Still, of the five Democratic presidents, only Carter cast more vetoes per year (and that by a very slight margin) than the average of 5.40 for all eight presidents serving during the 48-year period. Of the three Republican presidents, only Eisenhower's veto record fell below the overall average. Thus, Republican presidents serving from 1933 to 1981 were somewhat more likely to veto nationally significant bills than Democratic chief executives who were in office during that period.[17]

Table 2.4 shows no clear distinction in the tendency to veto significant legislation between presidents who had prior service as governor compared to those who had previously been in Congress. The latter were somewhat more inclined to veto than the former, but that tendency was attributable primarily to President Ford's vetoes. Of the other four presidents who previously served in the national legislature, only Nixon's veto record exceeded that

TABLE 2.4. Vetoes of Nationally Significant Legislation, 1933–1981, by Personal Background of President

|  | No. of Signif. Vetoes | No. of Years Served | Signif. Vetoes Per Year |
|---|---|---|---|
| **Party Affiliation** | | | |
| *Democrats* | | | |
| Roosevelt | 60 | 12.37 | 4.85 |
| Truman | 37 | 7.63 | 4.85 |
| Kennedy | 4 | 2.90 | 1.38 |
| Johnson | 9 | 5.10 | 1.76 |
| Carter | 22 | 4.00 | 5.50 |
| Total | 132 | 32.00 | 4.13 |
| *Republicans* | | | |
| Eisenhower | 34 | 8.00 | 4.25 |
| Nixon | 38 | 5.69 | 6.68 |
| Ford | 55 | 2.31 | 23.81 |
| Total | 127 | 16.00 | 7.94 |
| TOTAL | 259 | 48.00 | 5.40 |
| **Previous Office** | | | |
| *Governor* | | | |
| Roosevelt | 60 | 12.37 | 4.85 |
| Carter | 22 | 4.00 | 5.50 |
| Total | 82 | 16.37 | 5.01 |
| *Congress* | | | |
| Truman | 37 | 7.63 | 4.85 |
| Kennedy | 4 | 2.90 | 1.38 |
| Johnson | 9 | 5.10 | 1.76 |
| Nixon | 38 | 5.69 | 6.68 |
| Ford | 55 | 2.31 | 23.81 |
| Total | 143 | 23.63 | 6.05 |
| *Neither* | | | |
| Eisenhower | 34 | 8.00 | 4.25 |
| TOTAL | 259 | 48.00 | 5.40 |

of the overall record of all eight presidents of the period (5.40 vetoes per year). The two ex-governors, Roosevelt and Carter, were both fairly close to that overall average of vetoes per year, the former somewhat below and the latter slightly above it.[18]

## Presidential-Congressional Relations

When a president vetoes legislation, the action involves a conflict between him and Congress. This being the case, one might expect that general factors affecting presidential-congressional relations would affect the incidence of such vetoes. One such factor, or variable, is the partisan composition of Congress compared with the party affiliation of the chief executive. Woodrow Wilson, a general student of presidential-congressional relations, Mason, who analyzed vetoes in the last century, and Light, a modern student of the president's agenda, all refer to the fundamental importance of that matter.[19] Moreover, some previous studies include it in their statistical analyses of presidential vetoes.[20] A further refinement of that same factor is whether the degree of control of the Congress by the president's party, as represented by the percentage of the total seats it holds in the entire Congress, has an even more marked effect on presidential vetoes.[21]

Although the partisan factor contributes to presidential-congressional conflict, it does not completely shape it. Analyses of congressional roll-call voting in our system indicate that the party affiliation of members of the Congress is the most important single variable in such voting, but it is not completely determinative.[22] For example, since the late 1930s, Southern Democrats have been more likely to vote with Republicans in both houses than have

43

Northern Democrats.[23] It would be helpful, therefore, to explore other variables that might better reflect presidential-congressional conflict than partisanship.[24]

One such variable is how well or poorly a president does in persuading members of Congress to enact legislation he favors. Fortunately, the *Congressional Quarterly Almanac* had devised two measures of that influence. One is called the "presidential box score." It consists of the percentage of proposals the president requests each year either in messages to Congress or other public statements that are eventually enacted into law. That annual percentage figure is available from 1954 through 1975. The second measure, called the "presidential support score," indicates the percentage of congressional roll-call vetoes on which the president takes a clear stand and wins. (This measure is broader than the box score because it includes legislation the president favors even though he does not request it and it is also available from 1953 through 1980 rather than just through 1975 as is the box score.) A low score on either measure indicates that the president is having trouble getting Congress to enact legislation he requests or favors. This situation reflects major presidential-congressional conflict and might be expected, in turn, to result in an increase in presidential vetoes of measures that Congress passes.

A final dimension of presidential-congressional relations is a cyclical one that takes into account when such vetoes tend to occur. Presidents generally enjoy their greatest success in dealing with Congress during the so-called honeymoon period that occurs when they first take office. This being the case, one would expect presidents to find it less necessary to veto legislation during their first year in office than in the succeeding three years. The same tendency is true in relation to their terms in office.

Presidents are generally more successful in dealing with Congress during their first term, and that tendency should lead to a lower incidence of vetoes in first terms than in succeeding ones.[25]

As Table 2.5 indicates, a party's control of Congress does have a major effect on presidential vetoes. The chief executives serving in the 1933–1981 period cast more than twice as many vetoes per year when the opposition party controlled Congress as they did when their own party did. However, the degree of partisan control appears

TABLE 2.5. Effect of Certain Presidential-Congressional Variables on Vetoes of Nationally Significant Legislation, 1933–1981

| Variable | No. of Vetoes | No. of Years | Average Vetoes Per Year |
|---|---|---|---|
| *Control of Congress* | | | |
| Pres. party | 124 | 32 | 3.88 |
| Oppos. party | 135 | 16 | 8.44 |
| | 259 | 48 | 5.40 |
| *Percentage of Congressional Seats Controlled by Pres. Party* | | | |
| Below 50 | 135 | 16 | 8.44 |
| 50–66 | 75 | 22 | 3.41 |
| 67 or more | 49 | 10 | 4.90 |
| | 259 | 48 | 5.40 |
| *Pres. Box Score*[a] | | | |
| Below 40% | 61 | 8 | 7.63 |
| 40–49% | 49 | 9 | 5.44 |
| 50% and above | 10 | 5 | 2.00 |
| | 120 | 22 | 5.45 |

(*continued*)

TABLE 2.5. Continued

| Variable | No. of Vetoes | No. of Years | Average Vetoes Per Year |
|---|---|---|---|
| *Pres. Support Score*[b] | | | |
| 66% and below | 96 | 7 | 13.71 |
| 67–79% | 55 | 14 | 3.93 |
| 80% and above | 11 | 7 | 1.57 |
| | 162 | 28 | 5.79 |
| *Year of Term* | | | |
| 1 | 58 | 12.41 | 4.67 |
| 2–4 | 201 | 35.59 | 5.65 |
| | 259 | 48.00 | 5.40 |
| *Term* | | | |
| 1 | 153 | 25.94 | 5.90 |
| 2 | 92 | 17.69 | 5.20 |
| 3 | 14 | 4.00 | 3.50 |
| 4 | 0 | 0.37 | 0.00 |
| | 259 | 48.00 | 5.40 |

[a]Includes only years 1954 through 1975
[b]Includes only years 1953 through 1980

not to have been as important. Presidents in the 1933–1981 period vetoed more bills per year when their party controlled two-thirds or more of the seats in Congress than they did when their party's seat proportion was between one-half and two-thirds of the two chambers. One possible explanation for this fact is that presidents are more inclined to veto bills when they calculate that their strong party control of Congress makes it highly unlikely that their vetoes will be overridden by the necessary two-thirds vote in both chambers. Presidents may also be more cautious in using the veto and possibly making enemies when their party has a smaller advantage in Congress.

The table also indicates that presidential influence over Congress on bills chief executives requested or favored was inversely related to their tendency to veto legislation. As both presidential box scores and support scores increased, the average number of vetoes decreased. The progression was not only in the anticipated direction but also varied markedly from one level of presidential influence to another.

Finally, Table 2.5 shows that, as anticipated, presidents were somewhat less likely to veto legislation in the first than in the second, third, or fourth years of their terms. However, contrary to expectations, more presidential vetoes occurred in the first than in the second (or in Roosevelt's case, third and fourth) terms. The fact that the president who cast the most vetoes in the 1933–1981 period, Gerald Ford, served only one term, contributed to that situation.

*Standing with the American People*

Presidential vetoes represent a direct conflict between the chief executive and Congress, but the nature of that conflict may be affected by how well or poorly the president stands with the American people. The best measure of that standing is the public opinion polls taken by the Gallup organization that ask a cross-section of Americans whether they approve or disapprove of the way the president is handling his job. It is possible to average the results of the polls taken during a calendar year and use that figure as the presidential approval rating for that year. (The period covered in this analysis is from 1953 to 1981.) If as Neustadt suggests, members of Congress take into account the president's public prestige in deciding whether to give him what he wants, then when his polls are low, so will be his influence with Congress.[26] This development, in turn, should lead to a greater incidence of presidential vetoes.[27]

The electoral cycle may also affect presidential vetoes. One might expect the level of those vetoes to increase when politics becomes salient during mid-term congressional election years (when all members of the House and one-third of senators must face the voters) and again in presidential election years (when this group and the president face election).[28] If the incumbent president seeks reelection, that fact may also exacerbate political conflict between him and Congress and result in more presidential vetoes.[29]

As Table 2.6 indicates, variables relating to standing with the American public did affect the incidence of presidential vetoes in the ways that were anticipated. The lower the approval ratings of presidents, the more they resorted to vetoes. More vetoes also tended to occur in both congressional and presidential election years than in nonelection years. Finally, presidents who sought reelection tended to veto more legislation than did those who did not face the voters for another term.

## Nature of the Times

A final general factor that might be expected to affect the incidence of presidential vetoes is the nature of the times. Although many conditions affect relationships between the president, Congress, and the American people, two in particular are very important. One is our nation's involvement in foreign and military affairs. The other is the general state of its economy.

TABLE 2.6. Effect of Certain Public-Standing Variables on
Vetoes of Nationally Significant Legislation, 1933–1981

| Variable | No. of Vetoes | No. of Years | Average Vetoes Per Year |
|---|---|---|---|
| *Approval Rating*[a] | | | |
| Below 50% | 90 | 9.00 | 10.00 |
| 50–66% | 56 | 11.00 | 5.09 |
| 67% and above | 12 | 8.00 | 1.50 |
| | 162 | 28.00 | 5.79 |
| | | | |
| *Election Year* | | | |
| Congressional | 84 | 12.00 | 7.00 |
| Presidential | 81 | 12.00 | 6.75 |
| Neither | 94 | 24.00 | 3.92 |
| | 259 | 48.00 | 5.40 |
| | | | |
| *President Seeking Reelection* | | | |
| Yes | 192 | 31.04 | 6.19 |
| No | 67 | 16.96 | 3.95 |
| | 259 | 48.00 | 5.40 |

[a]Includes only years 1953 through 1980

In times of military crisis in particular, there is a
tendency for the American people to "rally around the
flag" and hence to support the major political figure, the
president.[30] Moreover, presidents generaly find it easier
to garner congressional support for their policies in foreign and military matters than in domestic ones, a situation some scholars have labeled the "two presidencies."[31]
Rohde and Simon suggest that military problems divert
the attention of presidents from domestic concerns in
which presidential-congressional conflicts are more common.[32] All these conditions should result in fewer presi-

dential vetoes when the nation is involved in a military
conflict than in peacetime.[33]

If there are problems in the domestic economy, one
might expect both the president and Congress to become
involved in developing programs and policies to deal with
them. Such a situation might well lead to conflict between
the two branches and a consequent increase in presidential vetoes. The two measures used to determine the
general state of the economy are the yearly unemployment and inflation rates, which together constitute what
is frequently referred to as the "misery index."[34]

Table 2.7 shows that the nature-of-the-times variables
were associated with presidential vetoes in the ways that

TABLE 2.7. Effect of Certain Nature-of-the-Times Variables on
Vetoes of Nationally Significant Legislation, 1933–1981

| Variable | No. of Vetoes | No. of Years | Average Vetoes Per Year |
|---|---|---|---|
| *Military Involvement* | | | |
| Yes | 62 | 15 | 4.13 |
| No | 197 | 33 | 5.97 |
| | 259 | 48 | 5.40 |
| *Rate of Unemployment* | | | |
| Below 5% | 70 | 20 | 3.50 |
| 5% and above | 189 | 28 | 6.75 |
| | 259 | 48 | 5.40 |
| *Rate of Inflation* | | | |
| Below 5% | 132 | 32 | 4.13 |
| 5% and above | 127 | 16 | 7.94 |
| | 259 | 48 | 5.40 |

were anticipated. The incidence of such vetoes was somewhat higher in years when the nation was not involved in military hostilities. Economic conditions, however, were more influential: Almost twice as many vetoes were cast in years when the unemployment and inflation rates exceeded the level of 5 percent.

Summarizing the above analysis, a range of factors affected the incidence of vetoes in the 1933–1981 period. Most relevant were congressional-presidential relations, standing with the American public, and the general nature of the times. The personal backgrounds of the eight presidents were not as important.

Although the analysis does suggest some factors related to the incidence of presidential vetoes from 1933 to 1981, it is deficient in several respects. First, it does not show how much each individual factor, or variable, affected the yearly variation in presidential vetoes. Second, it does not indicate the extent to which the individual variables were related to each other, and how that fact affected the independent effect each individual factor had on the variation in presidential vetoes. Finally, the analysis does not show the cumulative effect that different variables had on the variance in presidential vetoes.

The statistical device that measures such differences is multivariate time-series analysis. In this case, the dependent variable is the number of vetoes cast by presidents in equal time intervals, namely, the calendar year.[35] The various factors become the independent variables (also calculated on a yearly basis). The independent variables that are of an interval nature (such as the percentage of congressional seats held by the president's party) are expressed in those terms; those of a nominal nature (such as whether Congress was controlled by the president's party or by the opposition party) are cast in a binary fashion (1 or 0).

Having operationalized the data, I used a parsimonious approach to relate the independent variables to the dependent one. Specifically, a number of independent variables were analyzed to determine the least number of them that were each significantly related to the dependent variable and that combined had the greatest cumulative effect on that variable. Table 2.8 indicates that statistically three independent variables—presidential support score, election year, and the rate of inflation—were all closely related to the dependent variable of vetoes of nationally significant legislation. Of the three, the presidential support score variable was by far the most important. Nonetheless, the election year and inflation rates each exerted an additional effect on presidential vetoes. In other words, presidents were most likely to veto legislation when bills they favored were not being acted upon positively by the Congress. This situation was exacerbated during congressional and presidential election years and when the infla-

TABLE 2.8. Results of Multivariate Analysis of Vetoes of Nationally Significant Legislation, 1953–1981[a]

| Independent Variable | Standardized Beta Coefficient | Probability | T Ratio |
|---|---|---|---|
| Presidential support score | −0.6211 | 0.0001 | −5.508 |
| Election year[b] | 0.3064 | 0.0096 | 2.850 |
| Inflation rate | 0.2964 | 0.0186 | 2.567 |
| | | | |
| Adjusted R-Square | 0.7368 | | |
| Durbin-Watson | 2.0060 | | |
| N = 25[c] | | | |

[a]Only these years are included because presidential support scores were not available until 1953.
[b]Includes congressional and presidential election years.
[c]The N is 25 rather than 28 because in three years—1964, 1969, and 1979—there were no vetoes of nationally significant legislation.

tion rate was high, conditions that might be expected to increase conflict between the president and members of Congress concerned about their electoral fortunes and the best way to deal with economic conditions in the nation.[36] The table also shows that these three independent variables combined (adjusted $R^2$) explained almost three-fourths of the yearly variation in presidential vetoes over the 28-year period from 1953 to 1981.[37]

The analysis is helpful, but it has the disadvantage of being confined to the period beginning in 1953 when the presidential support score information provided by *Congressional Quarterly* first became available. It thus covers the presidential administrations beginning with that of Dwight Eisenhower and ending with the one of Jimmy Carter but omits those of Presidents Roosevelt and Truman (1933–1953). There is no reason to suppose that conditions affecting vetoes during those two presidencies were different from those of the subsequent six administrations, but the possibility exists.

In order to cover the entire era, 1933–1981, another multivariate time-series analysis was made, using those independent variables on which there was information for the entire 48-year period. Again a parsimonious approach was used to determine the least number of independent variables that were each significantly related to the dependent variable and that combined had the greatest effect on that variable. Table 2.9 shows that statistically four independent variables—percentage of congressional seats held by the president's party, election year, unemployment rate, and inflation rate—were all closely related to the dependent variable of yearly presidential vetoes over the entire period from 1933 to 1981. The most important variable is the percentage of congressional seats held by the president's party. However, a comparison with

TABLE 2.9. Results of Multivariate Analysis of Vetoes of
Nationally Significant Legislation, 1933–1981

| Independent Variable | Standardized Beta Coefficient | Probability | T Ratio |
|---|---|---|---|
| Percentage of seats | −0.5211 | 0.0004 | −3.896 |
| Election year[a] | 0.3610 | 0.0034 | 3.116 |
| Unemployment rate | 0.3896 | 0.0056 | 2.928 |
| Inflation rate | 0.2876 | 0.0194 | 2.436 |
| Adjusted R-Square | 0.4108 | | |
| Durbin-Watson | 1.1540 | | |
| N = 45[b] | | | |

[a]Includes congressional and presidential election years.
[b]The N is 45 rather than 48 because in three years—1964, 1969, and 1979—there were no vetoes of nationally significant legislation.

Table 2.8 indicates that it was not as closely related to vetoes of nationally significant legislation as was the presidential support score variable during the 1953–1981 period. As previously suggested, this may be attributable to the fact that voting does not occur in Congress only along party lines and also to the possibility that if the president's party controls more than two-thirds of the seats, he may be more inclined to cast vetoes he calculates will not be overridden. Moreover, the four independent variables (Table 2.9) combined (adjusted $R^2$) explain just over two-fifths of the yearly variation in presidential vetoes over the 48-year period (1933–1981) compared with almost three-fourths of the yearly variation associated with the three independent variables shown in Table 2.8 for the 28-year period (1953–1981).[38]

Despite these differences, the above analysis shows that the same general factors affected presidential vetoes in recent presidential administrations. Included were direct presidential-congressional conflicts, the salience of politics during congressional and presidential election years, and the state of the economy as represented by high rates of inflation and/or unemployment.[39]

In examining the kinds of legislation vetoed by presidents between 1933 and 1981, I again focus on public laws of national significance. There are two categories of such legislation. The first is legislation of the three general types passed by Congress—authorization, appropriation, and revenue. The second is legislation related to public policy.

*Authorization, Appropriation, and Revenue*

According to Plano and Greenberg, an authorization is "a legislative action that establishes a substantive program, specifies its general purposes and the means for achieving it, and indicates the approximate amount of money needed to implement the program."[40] To provide the money to carry out the program, Congress must enact a separate type of bill, called an appropriation, which often provides less than the full amount of funds permitted by the authorization legislation. Finally, revenue legislation raises the income designed to cover the appropriation of funds made by Congress. (In recent years revenues have not covered appropriations, and it has been necessary to borrow money to finance the deficit.)

One might expect more presidential vetoes of authorization legislation than appropriation or revenue bills. Many more authorization bills pass Congress each year than either of the other two types of legislation.[41] More-

55

over, because legislative bodies have historically been granted the "power of the purse," presidents might be inclined to defer to congressional wishes on measures raising and appropriating moneys. Finally, even if presidents would like to veto appropriation bills that contain provisions of which they disapprove, the absence of an item veto means that they must accept them if the programs and agencies affected by the provision of funds are to be able to continue to operate.

The vetoes of legislation of national significance cast between 1933 and 1981 generally reflected the above expectations. Ninety percent of them (232 of 259) were authorization measures. Eight percent of them (21 of 259) were appropriation bills. The remaining 2 percent (6 of 259) were revenue measures.

An analysis of vetoes of the latter two types revealed some interesting patterns. Republican Presidents Nixon and Ford cast 13 of the 21 vetoes of appropriation bills, primarily those affecting the Departments of Labor; Health, Education, and Welfare; and Housing and Urban Development. They also vetoed general appropriation bills that contained objectionable riders—in Nixon's case, the prohibition against using funds to bomb Cambodia, and in Ford's, similar prohibitions affecting the provision of funds to Turkey. With respect to revenue legislation, Democratic Presidents Roosevelt and Truman cast 4 of the 6 vetoes. FDR's historic one was a major tax bill that he said seemed designed to provide tax relief "not for the needy but for the greedy"; Truman vetoed 3 separate bills to reduce income tax payments.[42]

### Public Policy

Over the period from 1933 to 1981, much legislation representing many different areas of public policy was vetoed by Presidents Roosevelt through Carter. As an aid to classifying such legislation, I examined the categories of legislation that *Congressional Quarterly* utilized since 1945 when it first began publication. Although generally helpful, these categories were not consistent over time. Moreover, new types of legislation developed as Congress intervened more extensively into areas of public policy, such as energy and the environment, with which it had not previously been so involved. I adopted my own classification scheme to take account of these factors and ultimately formulated 25 categories.

Although these categories enabled me to focus on specific policy areas covered by the vetoed legislation, it was difficult to make significant generalizations because there were so many categories. I therefore attempted to develop a much smaller list of general categories of public policy into which the 25 specific policy areas could be grouped. I initially tried the categories of "distributive," "regulatory," and "redistributive," which were first developed by Theodore Lowi[43] and utilized more recently by Ripley and Franklin.[44] However, after experiencing difficulties in using these concepts, I decided to classify the vetoed legislation into subject-matter categories similar to those used by Aage Clausen.[45]

1. *Civil liberties and rights*
   Includes legislation relating to First Amendment freedoms, political participation, procedural safeguards in criminal proceedings, the right to privacy, as well as rights relating to equal treatment under the law.
2. *International involvement*
   Includes foreign aid, foreign trade, immigration and deportation, defense, and other general foreign policy matters.

3. *Social welfare*
   Includes legislation under which the federal government provides assistance to individuals and groups in such areas as agriculture,[46] health and science, education, welfare, housing, labor and manpower, area redevelopment, employment, and veterans' programs.
4. *Government management*
   Includes domestic legislation affecting the general public in the areas of energy, the environment and natural resources, public works, conservation, the internal organization of the federal government, its relations with states and localities, transportation, communication and commerce, general business, and the overall economy.

As with the analysis of vetoes of the three general types of laws passed by Congress (authorization, appropriation, and revenue), one might anticipate that more vetoes would apply to legislation involving some policy areas than to others. Because the social welfare and government management categories both cover such a broad range of special policy areas, one might expect vetoes to be most prevalent in those two areas. There should be fewer vetoes of laws involving international matters because less legislation is passed in that area and also because the "two presidencies" thesis previously referred to suggests that presidents are more likely to receive congressional support in foreign and military matters than in domestic ones. Finally, given the limited number of bills that are passed by Congress that affect civil liberties and civil rights, one might expect relatively few vetoes in that area of public policy.

An analysis of the vetoes by policy area confirmed the

above expectations. As shown in Table 2.10, of the 253 vetoes that were classified in that way (6 were general appropriation bills that could not be so categorized), nearly 42 percent (106 of 253) were in the social welfare domain and about 41 percent (104 of 253) involved the government management area. In contrast, approximately 14 percent (36 of 253) related to matters of international involvement and only about 3 percent (7 of 253) pertained to civil liberties and civil rights.

As far as vetoes by individual presidents are concerned, we might anticipate some differences among them. Clausen's analysis of voting in the House of Representatives by policy areas[47] indicates that Republicans tend to have a low level of support for both social welfare

TABLE 2.10. Vetoes of Nationally Significant Legislation, 1933–1981, by General Policy Area and by Party of President[a]

|  | Civil Liberties and Rights | International Involvement | Social Welfare | Government Management |
|---|---|---|---|---|
| *Republicans* | | | | |
| DDE |  | 4 | 10 | 20 |
| RMN | 1 | 2 | 19 | 15 |
| GRF | 2 | 10 | 23 | 18 |
| (Overall) | (3) | (16) | (52) | (53) |
| | | | | |
| *Democrats* | | | | |
| FDR | 1 | 7 | 35 | 15 |
| HST | 3 | 4 | 11 | 18 |
| JFK |  | 1 | 1 | 2 |
| LBJ |  | 2 | 1 | 6 |
| JC |  | 6 | 6 | 10 |
| (Overall) | (4) | (20) | (54) | (51) |
| Total | 7 | 36 | 106 | 104 |

[a]It was not possible to classify 6 of the general appropriation bills by policy area.

and government management legislation while Democrats have a high level of support for such legislation. At the same time, there is no appreciable difference between Republican and Democratic legislators in voting on bills in the areas of international involvement and civil liberties and civil rights. If presidents behave like their fellow partisans in the House of Representatives, then we might expect Republican chief executives to veto more social welfare and government management legislation than their Democratic counterparts. At the same time, there should be no appreciable differences between presidents of the two parties with respect to vetoes of bills related to international involvement and civil liberties and civil rights.

Table 2.10 does show some differences between Republican and Democratic presidents with respect to the incidence of vetoes affecting the areas of civil rights and civil liberties and international involvement. However, the differences are minor, especially when the limited number of vetoes in both areas is taken into account. Democratic chief executives cast 4 of the 7 vetoes relating to civil liberties and civil rights, and 3 of these 4 were cast by Truman.[48] Of the 36 vetoes relating to international involvement, 20 were by Democratic presidents and 16 by Republican ones; moreover, a Republican chief executive, Ford, was responsible for the most vetoes—10.

Expectations with respect to vetoes in the two most prevalent areas of public policy—social welfare and government management—were not borne out. Republican chief executives did not veto more legislation in these areas than Democrats; in both areas the vetoes were split evenly between them. Perhaps most surprising is the fact that a Democratic president, Roosevelt, cast the most vetoes in the social welfare field, one-third of the total of 106.

In investigating possible reasons for these unexpected results, I examined the specific policy areas in which presidential vetoes were cast. Of the 35 vetoes Roosevelt cast in the social welfare area, 34 were associated with two fields: 20 with agricultural subsidies and 14 with veterans' benefits.[49] The two Republican presidents, Ford and Nixon, who were next in terms of vetoes in the social welfare field, negated legislation in other specific areas, such as health and science, education, and labor, which drew fewer vetoes from Democratic chief executives.

An analysis of vetoes cast in the government management field by specific policy area also reveals differences between Republican and Democratic presidents. Republican vetoes were more likely to be concentrated in the fields of the environment and natural resources and public works; of the 35 vetoes cast in those two areas, 27 were by Republican presidents. In contrast, vetoes by Democratic chief executives tended to occur more in the fields of transportation, communication and commerce, and the overall economy; of the 21 vetoes in those two areas, 16 were by Democratic presidents.

Now that we have a picture in mind of vetoes cast in the period from 1933 to 1981, I turn to the process by which decisions were made on such vetoes.

## NOTES

1. It should be noted, however, that some public legislation, such as revenue bills, often contain what are referred to as "Christmas tree" provisions that benefit a relatively few individuals or groups. Thus, the basic distinction between public and private legislation, while important, is not absolute. One study focusing on vetoes of private legislation is Clarence A. Berdahl, "The President's Veto of Private Bills," *Political Science Quarterly*, 52 (December 1937): 505–531.

2. "Efforts to Reduce Private Legislation," *Guide to Congress,* 3d ed. (Washington, D.C.: Congressional Quarterly, Inc., 1982), p. 358.

3. Ibid., p. 359, citing Abraham Lincoln, "First Annual Message to Congress," in Fred L. Israel (ed.), *The State of the Union Messages of the Presidents, 1790–1966* (New York: Chelsea House, Robert Hector Publishers, 1966), 2:1060.

4. Ibid.

5. 370 U.S. 530 (1962).

6. For an analysis of that legislation and the situation that gave rise to it, see U.S. Congress, *Senate Congressional Cases,* U.S. Court of Claims, S. Rept. 1643, 89th Cong., 2d sess., September 22, 1966 (Washington, D.C.: Government Printing Office, 1966).

7. As a check on my subjective judgments on the matter, I compared my list of significant presidential vetoes cast since 1945 against vetoes discussed in the *Congressional Quarterly Almanac,* which began publication that year. I found in almost all cases that it covered the same vetoes as were on my list. When it did not, I resolved the matter in favor of inclusion of vetoes that appeared on either of the lists. John Woolley, "Institutions, Election Cycles, and the Presidential Vetoes," *American Journal of Political Science* 35 (1991): 279–302, who made a similar distinction, reported an agreement rate of 88 percent with my classification. For an example of a study that attempts to distinguish the important laws that were passed by Congress in recent years (not just those that were vetoed), see David Mayhew, *Divided We Govern: Party Control, Lawmaking, and Investigations, 1946–1990* (New Haven: Yale University Press, 1991), chap. 3.

8. It was assumed that Congress would not send important legislation to the president at the end of the session because a pocket veto would prevent its having an opportunity to override the veto. The assumption proved to be true; a check of the 68 pocket vetoes cast from 1945 to 1981 indicated that none of them pertained to bills that the *Congressional Quarterly Almanac* designated as involving a "key" vote. (The criteria used to determine a key vote is explained in the text.)

9. *Congressional Quarterly Almanac* (Washington, D.C.: Congressional Quarterly, Inc., 1986), 42:3C.

10. Other methods of taking votes in both chambers besides by roll-call are by voice or a standing vote. In addition, the House of Representatives traditionally employed teller votes in which members filed up the center aisle past counters, and only vote totals were announced. However, since 1971, one-fifth of a quorum can demand that the votes of individual members be recorded. Ibid., p. 16.

11. Harry S Truman, *Years of Trial and Hope.* Vol. 2 of *Memoirs* (Garden City: Doubleday and Company, 1956), p. 479.

12. Other historic vetoes included ones cast by Roosevelt of the Soldiers' Bonus bill of 1934, the Smith-Connally Anti-Strike bill of 1943, and the Revenue Act of 1944; Eisenhower's of the Natural Gas Act of 1956 (because of lobbying improprieties that caused him to veto it), and Nixon's veto of the War Powers Act of 1973.

13. Jong Lee, "Presidential Vetoes from Washington to Nixon," *Journal of Politics* 37 (1975): 522–546; Gary Copeland, "When Congress and the President Collide: Why Presidents Veto Legislation," *Journal of Politics* 45 (1983): 696–710; David Rohde and Dennis Simon, "Presidential Vetoes and Congressional Response: A Study of Institutional Conflict," *American Journal of Political Science* 29 (1985): 397–427, all focus on all vetoes of public bills, while Samuel Hoff, "Presidential Support in the Veto Process, 1979–1985" (Ph.D. Diss., University of New York–Stony Brook, 1987), chap. 2, examined only regular (not pocket) vetoes of public bills. As previously indicated, Woolley's study, "Institutions, Election Cycles, and the Presidential Vetoes," distinguished between major and minor public bills.

14. Lee, "Presidential Vetoes from Washington to Nixon," used a congressional rather than a calendar year as the unit of analysis, while Rohde and Simon, "Presidential Vetoes and Congressional Response," and Woolley, "Institutions, Election Cycles, and the Presidential Vetoes," utilized the legislative year. Copeland, "When Congress and the President Collide," and Hoff, "Presidential Support," used the calendar year.

15. Lee and Copeland use both the number of vetoes and the percentage of vetoes of public legislation as dependent variables. The results of each type of analysis are similar.

16. V. O. Key, Jr., *Politics, Parties, and Pressure Groups,* 5th ed. (New York: Thomas Y. Crowell, 1964), pp. 659f.

CHAPTER TWO

17. Lee, "Presidential Vetoes from Washington to Nixon,"
who analyzed presidential vetoes of all public bills passed from
the 21st through the 91st congresses (1829–1973), found Democratic presidents more likely to veto such legislation than Republican ones. However, Copeland, "When Congress and the
President Collide," who studied vetoes of such bills in the post–
Civil War period, as well as for our entire history, attributed
that tendency primarily to the large number of vetoes cast by
two individual presidents, Franklin Roosevelt and Grover Cleveland, rather than to Democratic presidents in general.

18. Lee, "Presidential Vetoes from Washington to Nixon,"
used the number of years served in the governorship or in the
national legislature as independent variables and found the
latter to be significant for the veto record of presidents.
Copeland, "When Congress and the President Collide," tested
only whether chief executives had ever served in Congress and
did not find that factor to be significant in his analysis.

19. Woodrow Wilson, *Congressional Government: A Study
in American Politics* (Boston: Houghton Mifflin, 1885), pp. 227ff.;
Edward Mason, *The Veto Power: Its Origin, Development, and
Function in the Government of the United States* (Boston: Ginn
Company, 1891), p. 126; and Paul Light, *The President's Agenda:
Domestic Policy Choice from Kennedy to Carter* (Baltimore:
Johns Hopkins University Press, 1982), pp. 27–28.

20. Lee, "Presidential Vetoes from Washington to Nixon,"
and Copeland, "When Congress and the President Collide." The
former distinguished between situations in which the opposition
party controls one or both houses of Congress, while the latter
took into account whether that party controls either body. This
difference was not an issue in this analysis because in the 1933–
1981 period, the opposition party controlled both houses simultaneously, or neither of them.

21. Rohde and Simon, "Presidential Vetoes and Congressional Response," and Hoff, "Presidential Support," utilized this
factor in their analysis while Lee, "Presidential Vetoes from
Washington to Nixon," and Copeland, "When Congress and the
President Collide," did not. Lee specifically made the assumption that "the threshold of majority is more important than the
absolute proportion of partisans" (p. 532).

22. One classic study that confirms this finding is Julius

Turner, *Party and Constituency,* rev. ed. by Edward Schneider (Baltimore: Johns Hopkins University Press, 1970).

23. The development of the Conservative Coalition is treated in James Patterson, *Congressional Conservatism and the New Deal* (Lexington: University of Kentucky Press, 1967). For a more recent analysis of the coalition, see David Brady and Charles Bullock III, "Coalition Politics in the House of Representatives," in Lawrence Dodd and Bruce Oppenheimer (eds.), *Congress Reconsidered,* 2d ed. (Washington, D.C.: Congressional Quarterly Press, 1981), pp. 186–203.

24. Two recent studies that explore not only partisan divisions but also geographical and ideological ones within Congress and their effect on its relationships with the president are George C. Edwards III, *At the Margins: Presidential Leadership of Congress* (New Haven: Yale University Press, 1989), chaps. 3 and 5, and Jon R. Bond and Richard Fleisher, *The President in the Legislative Arena* (Chicago: University of Chicago Press, 1990), chap. 7.

25. Hoff, "Presidential Support," found that both year and term affected the incidence of presidential vetoes. Copeland, "When Congress and the President Collide," determined that year was not significant in the post–Civil War period.

26. Richard Neustadt, *Presidential Power: The Politics of Leadership from FDR to Carter* (New York: Wiley, 1980), p. 64. It should be noted, however, that Neustadt recognized, "This is a factor operating mostly in the background as a conditioner, not the determinant, of what Washingtonians (which includes members of Congress) will do about a President's request" (p. 65). Two other recent analyses of the relationship between public approval of the president and congressional voting found the relationship to be marginal. See Edwards, *At the Margins,* p. 113, and Bond and Fleisher, *The President in the Legislative Arena,* p. 223.

27. Rohde and Simon, "Presidential Vetoes and Congressional Response," and Woolley, "Institutions, Election Cycles, and the Presidential Vetoes," found this to be the case.

28. Rohde and Simon, "Presidential Vetoes and Congressional Response," determined that congressional election years affected vetoes more than presidential ones did.

29. The assumption was made that the president's decision

to run for reelection affected that maneuvering throughout his term, which may not be the case if that decision was not predictable.

30. John Mueller, *War, Presidents, and Public Opinion* (New York: Wiley, 1973).

31. The thesis was initially stated by Aaron Wildavsky in "The Two Presidencies," *Trans-action* 4:2 (December 1966), 101–110. It has been generally confirmed in a number of more recent studies. For examples of other recent studies emphasizing the limitations on and conditions associated with the thesis, see Edwards, *At the Margins,* chap. 4, and Bond and Fleisher, *The President in the Legislative Arena,* chap. 6.

32. Rohde and Simon, "Presidential Vetoes and Congressional Response," p. 405.

33. Included were World War II and the Korean and Vietnamese hostilities. The previously cited studies by Copeland, Rohde and Simon, and Hoff all use essentially the same independent variable; Lee utilizes the number of armed forces per 1,000 population.

34. The economic indexes used in the studies previously referred to vary considerably. Lee utilized the wholesale price index; Copeland, general historical periods of economic downturn; Hoff, the level of unemployment; and Rohde and Simon, public attitudes toward the seriousness of economic as compared to other types of foreign, military, and noneconomic problems, as revealed by Gallup polls.

35. Because of the nonlinearity of the relationship between the independent variables and the dependent one, the log of the yearly vetoes was utilized. Lee, "Presidential Vetoes from Washington to Nixon," and Copeland, "When Congress and the President Collide," used the same approach.

36. A separate, multivariate analysis revealed that the rate of unemployment had a coefficient of .2277 with the dependent variable, which falls just short of the .05 level of significance (.0588 to be exact). When it is combined with the presidential support score and election year variables, the adjusted $R^2$ is .7095, slightly less than the .7368 figure shown in Table 2.8 that substitutes inflation rate for the unemployment one as the third independent variable.

37. Because President Ford cast so many of the vetoes over

that period (55 of 162), a test was run to determine whether he was an "outlier" that distorted the general situation during that 28-year period. This was done by creating a separate "dummy" variable for Ford and rerunning the data in Table 2.8. However, the analysis indicated that the Ford variable was not statistically significant, which means that the relationships previously discussed transcend the situation during the Ford administration. Woolley, "Institutions, Election Cycles, and the Presidential Vetoes," reports some effect of the Ford experience on his findings.

38. The test discussed in the previous note was also run for the analysis of the entire 1933–1981 period. It again showed that the statistical relationships were not attributable to the Ford presidency.

39. Other studies with similar time frames to this one found that some of the same kinds of independent variables were related to the incidence of presidential vetoes. Rohde and Simon, "Presidential Vetoes and Congressional Response," who analyzed vetoes of all public bills in the period from 1945–1981, identify as significant variables the president's approval rating, the proportion of congressional seats held by his party, congressional election years, the presence of international conflict, and the public's concern with economic problems. Woolley, "Institutions, Election Cycles, and the Presidential Vetoes," whose study builds on Rohde and Simon's but extends to 1986, also found the approval rating and seat proportion to be significant in the variation in the likelihood of vetoes of major legislation. Steven Schull and Dennis Gleiber, "Determinants of Presidential Veto Propensity" (Paper presented at the 1992 Annual Meeting of the Western Political Science Association, San Francisco, Calif., March 19–21), analyze vetoes from 1933 to 1988 and find presidential persuasion and presidential strength in Congress to be related significantly to the incidence of regular vetoes.

40. Jack Plano and Milton Greenberg, *The American Political Dictionary,* 7th ed. (New York: Holt, Rinehart, and Winston, 1985), p. 193.

41. In recent years, Congress has passed 600–700 public laws for a two-year Congress. The appropriations ones have been contained in 13 separate bills but at times, supplemental appro-

priations are required. Revenue bills are enacted periodically but not in a significant volume.

42. At the time of Truman's first veto of a tax bill, it was noted that Roosevelt's veto three years previously was the first of a general revenue bill in the nation's entire history, *New York Times,* June 16, 1947.

43. Theodore Lowi, "American Business, Public Policy, Case Studies and Political Theory," *World Politics* 16 (July 1964): 677–715.

44. Randall Ripley and Grace Franklin, *Congress, the Bureaucracy, and Foreign Policy,* 3d ed. (Homewood, Ill.: Dorsey Press, 1984).

45. Aage Clausen, *How Congressmen Decide: A Policy Focus* (New York: St. Martin's Press, 1973), especially chap. 3. Another study that attempts to classify presidential vetoes using Clausen's general approach is Albert Ringelstein, "Presidential Vetoes: Motivation and Classification," *Congress and the Presidency* 12, no. 1 (Spring 1985). However, his categories depart more from Clausen's than mine do.

46. Clausen uses agricultural assistance as a separate general policy area, but I have included it under the broad category of social welfare legislation.

47. Clausen, *How Congressmen Decide,* table 1, p. 107.

48. These included vetoes of two of the historic bills previously referred to—McCarron Internal Security and McCarran-Walter Immigration—along with one involving changes in the Hatch bill relating to political activities of public employees.

49. Agricultural benefits were a subject of presidential vetoes throughout the period of study, including 9 by Ford, which was second in frequency to Roosevelt's 20. In contrast, those involving veterans' benefits were concentrated in the early years: of the 21 vetoes cast in that specific policy area, 14 were by Roosevelt and another 4 by Eisenhower.

# 3

## EXECUTIVE BRANCH INFLUENCE
## ON PRESIDENTIAL VETOES

Although presidents are free to consult a variety of sources in deciding whether to veto a bill passed by Congress, it is natural that they turn to members of the executive branch for advice on such matters. At the time of Washington's first veto of an apportionment bill in 1792, he consulted his cabinet and found it divided, with Jefferson opposed to it and Hamilton recommending that the bill be approved.[1] Secretary of State Martin Van Buren was involved in writing Jackson's rejection of the Maysville internal improvement bill,[2] and Amos Kendall, auditor to the Treasury, wrote the first draft of Jackson's message vetoing the legislation rechartering the Bank of the United States.[3] In considering his first private relief bill, Grant consulted the chief of ordinance, Major General A. B. Dyer,[4] and based his veto on the letter he received from Dyer. Hoover ordered the Veterans' Bureau to conduct an investigation into the needs of veterans before he vetoed legislation that would have granted veterans compensation.[5]

During the Roosevelt administration, however, a more centralized and regularized process was established for gathering advice from executive officials on whether the president should veto legislation passed by Congress. The first section of this chapter traces the development of that process and the changes that occurred in it during the

CHAPTER THREE

administrations of Presidents Roosevelt through Carter.
The second section analyzes the recommendations of the
various executive agencies advising presidents on veto
decisions during those administrations and the extent to
which presidents followed those recommendations in exercising vetoes of public legislation of national significance during that time. The third section discusses the
development of the veto message.

THE DEVELOPMENT OF THE ADVISORY PROCESS

In the early years of the Roosevelt administration, the
practice continued of gathering advice on presidential
vetoes from a variety of executive sources. Jackson's account of presidential vetoes indicates that "Roosevelt kept
hundreds of people busy checking the legitimacy of the
relief and pension bills."[6] The president also sought the
recommendation of the attorney general, Homer Cummings, and the secretary of agriculture, Henry Wallace,
on the Agricultural Adjustment bill of 1934[7] and from the
attorney general and secretary of state, Cordell Hull, on
legislation passed that same year providing for the protection and preservation of domestic sources of tin.[8]

In late 1934, however, President Roosevelt initiated an
action that paved the way for the development of a more
systematic process for evaluating bills passed by Congress. He suggested in December of that year that the
practice of referring to the Bureau of the Budget prior to
presentation to Congress all proposals or views on legislation involving appropriations be supplemented by a process whereby all substantive legislation involving policy
matters first be sent to the president through the National Emergency Council. The following year by direc-

tion of the president, the bureau was made the clearance agency for legislation dealing solely with "fiscal" matters while those solely concerned with "policy" matters were to be referred to the National Emergency Council staff. The council went out of existence, and in late 1937, the bureau became the sole clearance agency for matters of both policy and finance. In 1938, the staff of the bureau was expanded to handle this function, which was placed in a separate Division of Coordination. Thus, a process evolved that enabled the bureau to coordinate the requests of executive agencies to be sure that they did not conflict and that they were in accordance with the president's own program. As Richard Neustadt, a close observer of the process, suggests, the new clearance process was seen "primarily as a means to keep the many-voiced executive from shouting itself down in the legislative process."[9]

Meanwhile a similar clearance process developed for assisting the president to make decisions on whether to veto enrolled bills passed by both houses of Congress. Since its establishment in 1921, the Bureau of the Budget had been asked for its view on enrolled appropriation bills. However, in 1934, Roosevelt requested that the bureau give its reaction to all private relief bills involving financial expenditures; the agency therefore developed a procedure whereby it sought and summarized the views of other concerned executive agencies. Soon the White House was also referring substantive public bills to the bureau, which circulated them to various agencies for their views. Beginning in 1936 all bills were sent to the bureau for clearance.[10]

This clearance process for enrolled legislation was facilitated by the use (for the first time) in 1938 of facsimile copies of enrolled bills that were sent directly to the bureau for circulation to concerned agencies. Meanwhile the original bill went back to Congress for signing by the speaker of the House and the vice president prior to its being sent on to the president. This enabled the bureau to begin the process of consideration of the bill prior to the ten-day period for the president's action on it; this period starts with the delivery to him of the original bill signed by the legislative leaders.

On January 19, 1939, under the direction of President Roosevelt, the bureau issued Circular 346 regularizing the procedure to be followed for enrolled legislation. It made the Bureau of the Budget the official presidential agency and required each executive agency involved in the process to reply to the bureau's request for an opinion within 48 hours; the reply was to include a recommendation backed by supporting information. Recommendations for a veto were to be accompanied by a draft veto message; if a pocket veto was recommended, a memorandum of disapproval was required.[11]

Thus, the two types of central clearance worked together to facilitate President Roosevelt's role as legislative leader. Neustadt explains the situation: "The Budget Bureau's work on agency proposals and reports built up a general comprehensive record, unmatched elsewhere in government, to buttress its consideration of enrolled bills. At the same time, its mandate on enactments now lent special point and purpose to clearance of measures in proposed and pending stages."[12]

With the formal process in place, institutions and roles were developed to provide advice to the president on enrolled legislation. Reorganization Plan 1 of April 25, 1939, transferred the Bureau of the Budget from the Treasury Department to the new Executive Office of the President.[13] The following year, the director of the budget bureau, Harold Smith, created five divisions in the agency, including one called Legislative Reference to assist in the coordination and clearance of enrolled bills (along with proposed legislation, executive orders, and proclamations).[14] Fred Bailey, who had worked in the bureau since its establishment, was placed in charge of the division and according to Wayne and Hyde, "saw his role as largely custodial and ministerial."[15] However, as Neustadt notes, although Bailey consistently took the position that "politics" was outside his province, "Budget recommendations would sometimes refer obliquely to 'other factors,' as a flag to the President, and sometimes agency reports would make more direct references to tactical considerations which went beyond the substantive pros and cons."[16]

Nonetheless, a separate type of review of enrolled legislation was needed because, as Neustadt points out, "The Budget Bureau did not represent or respond to the President on a closely personal and intimate basis. Someone was needed to help the President sift the flood of incoming bills in terms of the President's own predilections and 'feel' for situations, issues and personalities."[17] This function, traditionally one for the president's secretary, was assigned in 1939, when the White House got more additional staff, to one of the president's new administrative assistants, James Rowe, who examined every enrolled bill file. When Rowe left the White House in 1942, Samuel Rosenman, took over the responsibility of the newly created post of special counsel to the president. However, unlike Rowe, Rosenman did not analyze every enrolled bill file; rather, he confined his attention to those that seemed particularly important or had an "angle."[18]

Thus, two separate processes developed for reviewing enrolled bills: The bureau tended to look at substantive concerns and viewed legislation from the standpoint of the institutionalized presidency; the White House staff was atuned to political and personal considerations important to the president. When Rowe had any questions about the bureau's recommendations, he would consult informally with Bailey; disagreements between the two were taken directly to the president for resolution.[19]

The bureau generally served as the clearance agent on enrolled legislation; in some cases, however, agency heads went directly to the president or his aides with their recommendations. The administrator of the Office of Price Administration and Civilian Supply wrote to President Roosevelt urging him to veto a bill relating to wheat-marketing quotas under the Agricultural Adjustment Act of 1938.[20] The chairman of the Federal Security Agency sent a draft of a veto message relating to the social security amendment in a tax bill with the notation, "I thought you might have occasion to consider this matter before it comes to you in the routine manner."[21] Moreover, President Roosevelt sometimes solicited assistance directly from agency heads; he asked the attorney general to work up a draft veto message for the Walter-Logan bill in case it was passed and sent to the White House during his absence.[22]

### Continuation and Institutionalization

For a short period after President Harry Truman succeeded to the presidency in April 1945, the Bureau of the Budget lost its key role in legislative clearance to wartime agencies such as the Office of War Mobilization. (Neustadt quotes one highly placed Truman aide who remarked, "I simply do not see why legislative *policy* is any business of the *Budget* Bureau.")[23] However, the reappearance of domestic legislation as a key preoccupation; the decline or demise of other institutions, such as the War Mobilization Office; and the personality of James E. Webb, Truman's new director of the Bureau of the Budget, resulted by 1947 in the reemergence of the bureau as the major clearance agency.[24] This new clearance system affected not only the proposed and pending stages of the legislative process but operations on enrolled enactments as well.[25]

Personnel changes occurred in the Legislative Reference Division of the bureau when Bailey retired in 1947: Elmer Staats became assistant director for Legislative Reference, Roger W. Jones was his principal assistant, and Richard Neustadt was a key staff member.[26] However, the basic role that the division assumed in the enrolled bill process did not differ from the one it played in the Roosevelt administration. As Jones explains the situation, "He [President Truman] wanted institutional advice; he wanted someone to analyze for him the views of the departments, to give him the pros and cons, to stand aloof from the normal departmental attitude towards pieces of legislation, which heavily tended to reflect the department's constituency and to do objective analyses of the issues for the President."[27] Jones adds, "I've heard him [Truman] say many times, 'I will worry about the politics, you let me have it just as you see it from the policy, the programmatic, the substantive, point of view.'"[28] Neustadt sees the process essentially the same way: "Jones' attitude is that the Bureau's work on enrolled bills is a limited staff service, subject to review by the White House staff and to be complemented by separate White House staff work on political angles and outside considerations. Except in special circumstances, Jones thinks the Bureau can profitably stick to its limited role.

He is afraid of the consequences if the word gets around that the Budget is a stopping point on the lobby trail."[29]

Meanwhile, personnel changes also occurred in the White House operation. Rosenman left the White House in 1946, and the enrolled bill function remained with the Office of the Special Counsel, headed initially by Clark M. Clifford and later by Charles S. Murphy. The special counsel and his small staff interceded on a few major issues. As Clifford explains, "We were not equipped to do that job [review of enrolled bills] ourselves. Budget did it and did it effectively."[30] However, bureau people like Neustadt argue that in addition to that agency's review, "the President needs a review from his personal point of view as party leader and chief popular representative—this is met in part through the clearance process, with the participation of the Budget Director as a personal staff aid. In part it is furnished by additional screening in the White House as a matter of routine. In part it is not susceptible to any fixed procedure."[31]

The files of the Truman library do indicate that in the case of important legislation, the traditional review process for enrolled bills was not always followed. The White House did not ask the bureau to assemble views of executive agencies or give its own recommendation on HR 6042, a price-control bill; and in the case of another price-control bill, HJ Res. 371, representatives of various agencies concerned with the legislation, including the acting director of the budget, were called to a meeting at the White House to consider the enrolled bill.[32] President Truman also consulted members of his cabinet directly on legislation such as a bill to transfer federal lands to veterans,[33] the Case bill dealing with labor relations,[34] and the Taft-Hartley bill.[35] For the latter bill, Special Counsel Clark Clifford also consulted with experts in the Labor

Department and others outside the government.[36] Moreover, some agency heads contacted the president directly on matters of concern to them. The chairman of the Federal Power Commission wrote that although he had expressed no objection to the tidelands bill in his report to the director of the Bureau of the Budget, that action was taken in his official and ministerial capacity and that he personally recommended that the bill be vetoed.[37]

The election of Dwight Eisenhower in 1953 meant that a change of presidential administration also brought a change in the party controlling the White House. However, the enrolled bill process that had begun under Roosevelt and continued under Truman remained essentially the same during the Republican administration of Eisenhower. One factor that contributed to this result was Truman's action to prepare for the transition. As Neustadt describes the situation: "In 1951 Truman appointed as Budget Director a top Bureau careerist, Frederick J. Lawton, charging him specifically, though not publicly, to 'batten down the institution,' readying it for the transition." He explains: "The Bureau's reputation for 'nonpolitical' expertise, its institutional respectability, were to be guarded at all costs, thereby preserving its utility to the next President."[38]

Other factors also helped to perpetuate the essential nature of the enrolled bill process. Eisenhower, his senior aides, and the new budget director, Joseph M. Dodge, were all very favorably impressed with Roger Jones, who replaced Staats as head of Legislative Reference in 1949. As Wayne and Hyde explain, "Jones' personal influence, his policy orientation and obvious competence, combined with critical work his office was performing, explains in large part why the Eisenhower administration left the process basically intact."[39] Moreover, beyond a particular admiration for Jones, President Eisenhower and some of his senior aides were favorably disposed toward the Bureau of the Budget. Bryce Harlow, who had previously served in the Pentagon, and his superior, General Wilton Persons, a regular army officer, both had great respect for the bureau, as did the president himself, who had also been a career public servant.[40]

The White House role in the enrolled bill process also remained essentially the same as it had been in previous administrations. Chief of Staff Sherman Adams did not pass on most enrolled bill recommendations.[41] For the most part such matters were left to the special counsel to the president, Bernard Shanley, who depended on Jones and his successor, Philip Hughes, to do the analytical work on most enrolled legislation. The White House simply did not have the staff necessary to carefully scrutinize such legislation.

However, as in previous administrations, political considerations involved in particular legislation did affect the process somewhat. The bureau was not completely insensitive to political issues. Hughes remembered that on a bill involving benefits for black veterans, the bureau recommended a veto because it was a bad bill, "knowing full well that no one wanted to be in a position of vetoing a bill like that."[42] Harlow also stated that on one occasion the bureau wanted President Eisenhower to veto a bill that all agreed under the criteria of fairness should have been signed simply because it would set a "precedent"; Harlow replied that there "are good precedents and bad precedents" and influenced Eisenhower to sign the bill.[43]

Eisenhower also met with his cabinet more extensively than other presidents and on occasion used such meetings to discuss enrolled legislation. Most prominent in that regard was the controversy over a natural gas bill

78

that the president favored on its merits but which he ultimately vetoed because of alleged improprieties in lobbying on its behalf by certain oil companies, including the offer of a $2,500 bribe to Senator Francis Case of South Dakota. All sides of the issue were aired at a cabinet meeting, with administration officials divided on the issue.[44] A similar discussion also occurred with respect to a pay-raise bill at a cabinet meeting over which Vice President Nixon presided.[45]

The 1960 election of John Kennedy again involved a partisan change in presidential administration, but the enrolled bill process changed very little. Philip Hughes remained on as director of the Legislative Reference Division and dealt primarily on such matters with Kennedy's deputy special counsel, Myer Feldman, rather than with Theodore C. Sorensen, the president's special counsel. The only new development was that White House contacts with members of Congress increased as a result of Lawrence O'Brien's congressional liaison operation, with Feldman also acting as a channel for congressional views.[46]

When Lyndon Johnson succeeded to the presidency on the death of Kennedy, the enrolled process remained essentially intact as the key persons remained the same, with Hughes acting for the Bureau of the Budget and Feldman for the White House. However, Wayne and Hyde report that the Johnson administration sought a greater variety of views before making a decision.[47] This tendency is reflected in materials pertaining to Johnson's veto of a bill requiring that imported articles be marked with the name of the country of origin. Feldman sought individual opinions from the Office of the Special Representative for Trade Negotiation[48] and the Interior Department[49] and wrote a special memorandum to the president recommending a veto of the legislation.[50]

## Specialization and Politicization

After Lyndon Johnson was elected in his own right in 1964, changes began to occur that had the effect of altering markedly the nature of the enrolled bill process. Early in the administration, Philip Hughes left the Legislative Reference Division and was replaced by Wilfred S. Rommel. The only lawyer to serve in that capacity, Rommel viewed his role somewhat differently than his predecessors had. His advice on enrolled bills tended to be somewhat more legalistic and his memoranda to the president more technical and detailed. At the same time, he did not share the attitude of Jones and Hughes that careerists should play an aggressive role in advising the president on policy implications of legislation. As a result, Legislative Reference's influence on presidential veto decisions was reduced.[51]

Meanwhile, developments in the White House augmented its influence in the enrolled bill process. Harry McPherson, who became special counsel to the president in 1966, had to share his advice on such matters with Joseph Califano, Jr., who was placed in charge of domestic policy development and coordination in the Johnson White House and who eventually became involved in veto decisions as well. Because Califano's staff was larger and more specialized than McPherson's, his influence increased as time went on.[52]

On important legislation with political overtones, Johnson was not content to depend just on the counsel of Califano and McPherson. In the case of the District of Columbia crime bill, which provided for a number of controversial means of dealing with the rising crime rate in the nation's capital, Johnson sought advice from a variety of sources. A special assistant for District of Columbia affairs prepared a memorandum emphasizing the political history of the bill, including congressional voting on it, as well as the reaction of news media, party organizations, and interest groups to the bill.[53] Advice was also sought on the matter from persons outside the White House including D.C. attorney and former White House counsel, Clark Clifford, and associate justice of the Supreme Court, Abe Fortas, who advised Johnson to veto the bill.[54] (Johnson did not like the fact that vetoing the bill made him appear to be "soft-hearted" on crime but eventually accepted their counsel on the matter.)[55]

Toward the end of the Johnson administration, a new development in the internal organization of the Bureau of the Budget brought further charges in the enrolled bill process. A new political post, assistant director of human resources, was created, and its occupant began to establish direct contact with members of the White House staff on bills in the field of human resources. This created a separate channel of communication between policy specialists in the two organizations. This development, along with Rommel's inclination not to inject himself in policy matters unless he was asked to do so, served to reduce the influence of the Legislative Reference Division and its career civil servants on presidential decisions regarding bills passed by Congress.[56]

The election of Richard Nixon in 1968 again brought a partisan change in presidential administration and some further changes in the review process. Reorganization Plan 2 of 1970 changed the Bureau of the Budget to the Office of Management and Budget (OMB). Within the new OMB, four new political appointees called associate directors were installed; the associate directors were assigned policy and program responsibilities and reported to the director of OMB and his deputy. The same plan also created a Domestic Council within the White House office. The staff of this council reviewed all domestic legislation, including enrolled bills, and forwarded their recommendations to the director of the council, John Ehrlichman.[57]

These new structures in both OMB and the White House changed the earlier, traditional method for reviewing enrolled bill legislation. The policy specialists in both organizations met directly with each other, cutting the Legislative Reference Division out of the process. Moreover, the director of OMB, George Shultz, began signing all enrolled bill memoranda that contained veto recommendations.[58]

The changes outlined above served to politicize the process. The director of OMB was more concerned with "politics in the real world" than were career civil servants in the Legislative Reference Division.[59] For example, Director Shultz stated in one memorandum to the president recommending a veto of a bill dealing with the Federal Employees Pay System that some officials of the administration strongly opposed the bill and that he had warned others repeatedly of the possibility of a veto;[60] in another instance, he advised the same action on the Accelerated Public Works bill and referred to the fact that many Republican representatives and senators had supported the administration position in anticipation of a veto.[61] When Shultz left office and Caspar Weinberger became the director of OMB, he also noted similar political considerations, such as the possibility of an override of the Water Pollution bill by the two houses of Congress[62] and the original vote in the House of Representatives of 373 to 4 on the Research on Aging Act of 1972.[63] Similar factors were contained in memoranda to the president from Weinberger's successor, Roy Ash. He recommended a veto of the Small Business Administration Loan Ceiling and Disaster Loan amendments, noting that 167 House members supported the administration's opposition to loan forgiveness and that veto signals from several executive agencies were well known to Congress during its deliberations.[64] He also noted the presence of a clear veto signal to Congress if certain provisions were not removed from the War Powers Resolution.[65]

Moreover, the role of the White House in the enrolled bill process became more politicized. For example, a memorandum for the president through John Ehrlichman on the Hill-Burton bill on medical facilities construction noted that a copy of the memo was being referred to Bill Timmons, the head of the Congressional Liaison Office, for his assessment of congressional reaction.[66] Apparently this was a general practice as congressional opinion was inserted by the head of the liaison office, who automatically received a copy of all enrolled bills.[67]

After Nixon was reelected in 1972, changes in the White House operation continued to occur. Three new counselors to the president also known as "super secretaries" were created, and their staffs were supposed to take over some of the former responsibilities of the Domestic Council. However, this controversial new structure collapsed when its executive director, John Ehrlichman, was forced to resign on April 30, 1973, and was replaced by the deputy director of the agency, Kenneth Cole. OMB, under the aggressive leadership of Roy Ash, moved in to fill the vacuum and maintained a strong role in the latter part of the Nixon administration.[68]

When Richard Nixon resigned the presidency in August 1974 and Vice President Gerald Ford assumed the office, the role of OMB in the enrolled bill process remained essentially the same. Roy Ash stayed on for a period as director of the agency and continued to sign all veto recommendations of OMB. In some cases, he also sent a personal memorandum to the president suggesting he veto a particular bill such as one creating a new Federal Fire Administration.[69] His successor, James T. Lynn, also provided personal views to the White House, including responding to a request for a list of potential vetoes during a session of Congress.[70] Meanwhile, direct contacts between policy specialists of OMB and the Domestic Council on enrolled bills continued; also, at times, Lynn and his deputy, Paul O'Neill, met with the Domestic Council staff.[71] These practices continued to lessen the influence of career civil servants in the Legislative Reference Division, including Wilfred Rommel and his successor, James Frey.

Meanwhile, important changes were occurring in the Domestic Council in the Ford administration. Nelson Rockefeller was confirmed as vice president in December 1974, and in February 1975, President Ford decided to appoint him vice chairman of the Domestic Council. At the same time, Ford revealed the appointment of a Rockefeller aide, James Cannon, as the executive director of the council replacing Kenneth Cole. However, in practice all paperwork was channeled through the office of the assistant to the president for White House operations, Donald Rumsfeld, or his aide, Richard Cheney. Rockefeller became frustrated with his lack of control over day-to-day activities and lack of progress on long-range planning and asked in December 1975 to be relieved of his nominal leadership of the Domestic Council.[72]

Throughout the Ford administration, the two executive directors of the Domestic Council, Cole and Cannon, collected the views of various White House officials on enrolled bills. For each bill, they wrote a memorandum to President Ford reporting the views of those officials, and their own recommendations. Thus, they served a function in the White House similar to that OMB provided with respect to views of executive agencies. The council memoranda, however, tended to be shorter and somewhat more political in nature than the OMB ones. For example, in his memorandum on a bill providing for support of milk prices, Cole noted that the president had received communications from various representatives favoring the bill and that dairy farmers also strongly supported it.[73] Similarly, in his memorandum on a health services and nurse training bill, Cannon drew attention to the vote on the bill in both houses of Congress and stressed the fact that Senate Republican leaders favored the bill and that House Republican leaders reported that it would be difficult to sustain a veto.[74]

Although Cole and Cannon played a formal role in the enrolled bill process, they did not have the influence with President Ford that Ehrlichman had enjoyed with President Nixon. One member of the Domestic Council described the body as a kind of "executive secretariat," a collector of information more than a policy initiator or even coordinator.[75] Another high White House official described it as a "point of access" for cabinet members and as a "sounding board" for those who were opposed by OMB.[76] Contributing to the difficulties of Cannon in influencing veto decisions was the fact that he was considered a "Rockefeller person" and thus suffered when the vice president's influence declined in the Ford administration.[77]

An analysis of the legislative case files of the Ford administration reveals that the views of a wide variety of executive officials were sought on veto decisions.

Particularly prominent were close White House aides Phil Agreeda, Phil Buchen, Robert Hartman, Kenneth Lazarus, Jack Marsh, William Seidman, and speech writer Paul Theis. Also, congressional reaction was routinely solicited through Max Friedersdorf, head of the Office of Legislative Affairs, and on occasion, William Baroody, assistant to the president for public liaison, was asked to comment on legislation if interest group activity was particularly pronounced on it. If economic matters were involved, Alan Greenspan, chairman of the Council of Economic Advisers, and personal advisers Roger Porter and William Seidman were typically consulted, while foreign and military concerns were referred to the National Security Council for recommendations.

Rather than depending on written recommendations regarding vetoes as Richard Nixon did, President Ford preferred to hear different points of view presented and argued during staff meetings.[78] Moreover, the president actually read many of the bills himself and would note problems with them.[79]

Jimmy Carter's victory over Ford in the 1976 election again meant a change in the party controlling the presidency. However, there were no major changes in the way OMB handled the enrolled bill process. James McIntyre, who became director of OMB after Bert Lance was forced out of office early in the administration, continued the trend established by his immediate predecessors of personally signing all OMB memoranda recommending a veto of legislation.[80] In these memoranda McIntyre took particular note of the situation in Congress with respect to the legislation. He included not only such information as the vote on the original passage of the bill[81] but also the objection to pending legislation that OMB expressed to congressional committees prior to its enactment[82] and the necessity of working intensively to get Congress to sustain a veto.[83]

In some instances, McIntyre also wrote a separate personal memorandum to President Carter explaining special political considerations involved in a particular bill.[84] Beyond recommendations on specific legislation, he also wrote a memorandum to President Carter dealing with a general approach to veto decisions. In it he recommended that in addition to disapproving bills that raise major issues of public policy, including fiscal policy, the president should also veto some "narrow interest" legislation as a means of avoiding precedents that might cause problems in the future and also as a "very useful disciplinary example both to the agencies and the Hill."[85]

In the Carter White House, members of the domestic council staff were redesignated the domestic policy staff, but as in recent administrations, they continued to deal with program associate directors in OMB. However, there was no formal clearance process eliciting views of high executive officials as had developed in the Ford administration. Rather, Stuart Eizenstat, presidential assistant and head of the domestic policy staff, became the central figure in the enrolled bill process with other White House "generalists," such as David Rubenstein and Bert Carp, also looking at the overall picture affecting legislation passed by Congress. In addition, specialists in areas of public policy such as energy and housing were asked for their views on legislation in their particular domain.

The Carter White House was particularly sensitive to the general political climate of the times, including the fact that for the first time since the Johnson administration the same party controlled both the presidency and Congress. The head of congressional liaison, Frank Moore, joined with Eizenstat and McIntyre in developing a general "veto strategy" and a possible list of "veto candidates" to assist the president in the delicate situation of dealing with a supposedly friendly Congress and, at the same time, utilizing the veto as a "legitimate weapon in [his] legislative arsenal."[86] Strategy was also developed for dealing with Congress if a defense authorization bill were vetoed, including the formation of a coordinating team to try to prevent Congress from overriding the veto.[87] Following a veto, Public Liaison Aide Ann Wexler arranged a briefing of business executives and ethnic group leaders to explain the reasons for the veto,[88] and Media Adviser Gerald Rafshoon suggested that the entire cabinet and White House staff help educate the public on the matter by making speeches and TV and radio appearances and by contacting the administration's favorite columnists and news media representatives.[89]

With the development of the executive branch advisory process in mind, I now turn to an analysis of the recommendations of various agencies and the effect these recommendations have had on presidential veto decisions.

## ANALYSIS OF EXECUTIVE AGENCY RECOMMENDATIONS

Presidential decisions on enrolled bills follow the consideration of legislation by the executive branch. As previously indicated, the central clearance process that has been utilized since the Roosevelt administration begins with the Legislative Reference Division's assisting the administration in identifying and preparing the president's legislative program, including a compilation of "administration-sponsored" legislation. The division also facilitates executive branch clearance of all agency legislative proposals as well as agency testimony and reports on legislation pending in Congress. The division subsequently monitors the status of major legislation in Congress, focusing particular attention on administration-sponsored legislation and bills that deviate substantially from administration policy. Further, each week when Congress is in session, the division prepares a brief statement of the administration's position on each bill scheduled for House or Senate floor action.[90] Thus, when the time comes for final presidential action on bills passed by Congress, the Legislative Reference Division and other executive agencies are already well aware of the nature of the legislation and how it relates to the policies of the administration.

The process for the consideration of enrolled bills is also spelled out in detail by the division.[91] Facsimiles of all such bills are sent to the division, which identifies the agencies whose views and recommendations should be sought and sends a facsimile to each. (These are usually agencies that were involved in the clearance process, but the division errs on the side of including a greater number of agencies in order to give the president the benefit of as broad a range of views as possible.)[92] Agencies are to respond in writing within two days. Meanwhile, the White House is to notify the division of the formal receipt of the original bill, which officially begins the president's ten-day period for action on it. After receiving the views of the agencies and analyzing the content of the bill and committee reports and floor debates, the Legislative Reference Division prepares a memorandum for the president. It includes the subject of the bill, its congressional sponsor or sponsors, the last day for presidential action, the bill's purpose, the recommendations of agencies whose views were sought, and a discussion of the legislation's pros and cons; all of this is accompanied by the recommendation of OMB for approval or disapproval and a signing statement, if appropriate, or a veto message, if needed. The file on the bill containing all relevant information is sent to the White House by the fifth day of the president's ten-day period for action.[93]

Agencies recommend one of several actions on enrolled bills: "approval" (the president should sign the bill) or "disapproval" (the president should veto it); in addition, an agency is also permitted to "defer" to the advice of other executive agencies, to "voice no objection" to the bill, or to "take no position" on it. These latter three responses indicate that the agency does not feel that its interests are significantly affected by a particular bill, and in essence it takes a "neutral" view with respect to it.

There are three types of agencies whose views are solicited on enrolled bills. The first is the Office of Management and Budget (formerly the Bureau of the Budget), which is officially involved in making recommendations on virtually all legislation passed by Congress.[94] The second is known as the "lead" agency, that is, the one whose activities are most affected by an enrolled bill. The third includes "nonlead" agencies whose views are also sought on legislation.

One might anticipate different reactions to enrolled bills from these three types of agencies. As the guardian of the president's general interests, with a particular concern that legislation be "in accord with" or "consistent with" his legislative program and budget, and that it not establish an unfortunate precedent, OMB should be most inclined to recommend a veto of legislation. In contrast, the lead agency might be expected to be more favorable to enrolled bills that serve to increase its activities, jurisdiction, budget, and staff and to benefit its particular clientele. One might also anticipate that a kind of "logrolling" process would operate so that nonlead agencies would be somewhat inclined to either approve legislation or to be neutral toward it with the thought that other agencies would take that same stance on bills for which it is the lead agency.

A recent analysis by Wayne, Cole, and Hyde of executive agency recommendations on controversial enrolled bills during the Nixon and Ford administrations confirms these general expectations.[95] The lead agency advised the president to approve 56 percent of the bills compared with only 34 percent for OMB. The analysis also showed that when both OMB and the lead agency agreed that the legislation should be either approved or disapproved, the president was inclined to follow their joint advice. Moreover, if a majority of nonlead agencies also opposed legislation, the chief executive was even more likely to veto it.

My analysis differs from that of Wayne, Cole, and Hyde in two respects. It is broader in terms of presidential administrations, covering the period from Roosevelt through Carter.[96] However, it is narrower in terms of the type of presidential decision made because it is restricted to vetoes and does not include approvals of enrolled bills. Thus, one would expect to see a higher percentage of agency recommendations for disapproval than Wayne, Cole, and Hyde find from all controversial enrolled bills passed during the Nixon and Ford administrations, including those that were approved by the president.

Table 3.1 confirms my expectations with respect to recommendations of the three types of executive agencies. OMB recommended that only 3.3 percent of the vetoed bills be approved by the president as compared with 16.9 percent for the lead agency and 23 percent for the majority of the nonlead agencies. Moreover, OMB took a

TABLE 3.1. Agency Recommendations on Vetoed Legislation of National Significance

| Agency | Type of Recommendation (in percent) | | | Number[a] |
|---|---|---|---|---|
| | Approve | Disapprove | Neutral | |
| OMB | 3.3 | 93.8 | 2.9 | 210 |
| Lead agency | 16.9 | 74.4 | 8.7 | 207 |
| Nonlead agency[b] | 23.0 | 58.3 | 8.0 | 187 |

[a]The number varies because of differences in availability of agency recommendations. For example, on 20 vetoes of legislation, there was a lead agency recommendation but none for nonlead agencies. Also, the OMB report on one appropriation bill affecting a variety of agencies gave no indication which was the lead one, so the distinction on that bill was omitted from the analysis.
[b]These represent the recommendations of a majority of the nonlead agencies. In addition, for 10.7 percent of the vetoes (not shown above), the agency recommendations of approval and disapproval were evenly divided.

"neutral" position on an even smaller proportion of vetoed bills (2.9 percent) while both the lead and nonlead agencies took that position on more than twice that proportion of vetoed bills (8.7 percent and 8 percent, respectively). Thus, OMB did tend to recommend disapproval on nationally significant legislation more often than other executive agencies and to also take a stand rather than remain neutral more often than other agencies did on such legislation.

The analysis of agency recommendations showed some differences among presidential administrations. Of the 7 instances in which the chief executive vetoed a bill approved by OMB (3.3 percent of 210), 4 occurred during the Ford years. Richard Nixon was most inclined to veto legislation approved by the lead agency (30.3 percent), while among presidents with a significant number of vetoes, Ford was most likely to go against the advice of a majority of nonlead agencies that he sign such bills (27.7 percent).[97]

Finally, I analyzed the recommendations of executive agencies by the general division suggested by Thomas Cronin for cabinet departments, those of an "inner" versus an "outer" nature.[98] The first group, consisting of State, Defense, Treasury, and Justice, maintains a role as counselor to the president and represents broad-ranging, multiple interests.[99] The ones in the latter group, consisting of the remaining domestic policy departments, typically adopt the role of advocate for the particular clientele they represent (agriculture, business, labor, and the like).[100] I expected to find that the counseling, broad-interest orientation of the inner executive agencies would lead them to be less likely to approve of enrolled bills affecting their interests than would the outer executive agencies with their advocate orientation on behalf of their particular clientele.

Table 3.2 indicates that there were some differences in recommendations on vetoed bills by inner and outer lead agencies. As a group, the former approved of 14 percent of the vetoed bills as compared to 19.3 percent for the latter. However, there were major variations among the agencies within each of the two major categories. In the inner group, both the State and Defense departments recommended that almost one-quarter of the vetoed bills be approved and seldom took a neutral position on such bills; in contrast, the Justice and Treasury departments recommended that only about one-twentieth of the bills be approved but took a neutral position on almost one-quarter of such bills. As far as outer agencies were concerned, Health, Education, and Welfare, together with the Federal Security Agency, recommended that 30 percent (6 of 20) of

TABLE 3.2. Lead Agency Recommendations on Vetoed
Legislation of National Significance by Type of Agency

| Type of Agency[a] | Type of Recommendation (in percent) | | | |
|---|---|---|---|---|
| | Approve | Disapprove | Neutral | Number |
| *"Inner"* | | | | |
| State | 23.1 | 69.2 | 7.7 | 13 |
| Defense | 23.5 | 70.6 | 5.9 | 17 |
| Justice | 6.2 | 68.8 | 25.0 | 16 |
| Treasury | 5.6 | 72.2 | 22.2 | 18 |
| Others | 13.8 | 79.3 | 6.9 | 29 |
| Total | 14.0 | 73.1 | 12.9 | 93 |
| *"Outer"* | | | | |
| Agriculture | 19.2 | 69.2 | 11.5 | 26 |
| Commerce and Transportation | 0.0 | 100.0 | 0.0 | 17 |
| Interior | 16.7 | 75.0 | 8.3 | 12 |
| HEW-Fed. Sec.[b] | 30.0 | 70.0 | 0.0 | 20 |
| Other | 23.1 | 71.8 | 5.1 | 39 |
| Total | 19.3 | 75.4 | 5.3 | 114 |

[a]Agencies named are those that were involved in recommendations of at least 10 vetoed bills.
[b]Originally the Federal Security Agency was an independent agency, but later it became a part of the Social Security Agency which was, in turn, absorbed by the Department of Health, Education, and Welfare.

vetoed bills be affirmed, while together, the Commerce and Transportation departments made no recommendation of approval at all. It should also be noted that the combined approval recommendation of "other" agencies (included in Table 3.2) in the outer category occurred on almost one-quarter of vetoed bills; those with the highest proportion of approval recommendations were the Veterans' Administration and the Corps of Army Engineers, each of which recommended that the president approve half of the vetoed bills (3 of 6 and 2 of 4, respectively).[101] This type of recommendation accords with the general reputation of these agencies as serving a particularly assertive clientele.[102]

## THE VETO MESSAGE

The final step in executive branch influence on regular presidential vetoes is the development of the official message the president delivers in connection with his decision not to approve an enrolled bill. Under the provisions of the Constitution (Article I, Section 7), if the president fails to sign a bill presented to him, he is to return it "with his objections to that House in which it shall have originated, who shall enter the objections at large in their Journal and proceed to reconsider it." (In the case of pocket vetoes, which Congress has no opportunity to override, the president can choose to issue a memorandum of disapproval indicating his objections to the bill but he is not required to do so.)

A number of executive branch agencies and individuals are involved in developing the content of the official veto message. Agencies to which an enrolled bill is referred by OMB are requested to include a draft of a veto message for legislation that they recommend the president disapprove. In some cases, agencies join efforts and submit a suggested message that reflects their combined views.[103] The Legislative Reference Division takes the draft messages into account but often suggests its own version of a veto message, one that may include separate objections from different agencies and one that may also raise additional objections to the bill than those voiced by such agencies. The director of OMB may also offer suggestions. Persons on the White House staff may also rework the message, frequently to underscore "considerations" that may not have been as salient to the regular executive agencies, the Legislative Reference Division, or the director of OMB. Finally, the president may make changes of his own in the veto message or even write the entire message himself as Franklin Roosevelt did in connection with a "baby bond" bonus bill, which he vetoed in 1936.[104]

Generally, the written message is delivered to the house in which the vetoed bill originated; that body then begins deliberations on what course of action to take with respect to it. However, on some occasions the president chooses a more dramatic means of presenting his message. In 1935 Roosevelt delivered his veto message of the Patman Bonus bill to a joint session of Congress, the first president in history to do so.[105] In 1947 Truman explained his veto of the Taft-Hartley bill to the American people in a nationwide radio address.[106] Richard Nixon went on television in 1970 to give his reasons for vetoing an appropriation bill for the departments of Labor and Health, Education, and Welfare.[107]

### NOTES

1. Carlton Jackson, *Presidential Vetoes, 1792–1945* (Athens: University of Georgia Press, 1967), p. 2.

2. Ibid., p. 17.

3. Working over Kendall's draft was Jackson's private secretary, Andrew Donaldson, Attorney General Roger Taney, and Secretary of the Navy Levi Woodbury. Jackson himself passed in and out of the room, listening to the different parts of the redrafts, weighing the various suggestions and directing what should be inserted or altered. Arthur Schlesinger, Jr., *The Age of Jackson* (Boston: Little, Brown and Company, 1953), pp. 89f.

4. Jackson, *Presidential Vetoes,* p. 132.

5. Ibid., p. 191.

6. Ibid., p. 205.

7. Letter dated January 23, 1934, from Rudolph Forster, Executive Clerk, to Attorney General Homer Cummings, also referring to a report from the Secretary of Agriculture. OF 5708, Bureau of the Budget Enrolled Public Bills, Franklin D. Roosevelt Library.

8. Letter dated June 25, 1934, from Louis Howe, Secretary to the President, to Attorney General Homer Cummings; letter dated June 26, 1934, from Marvin H. McIntire, Assistant Secretary to the President, to Secretary of State Cordell Hull, OF 5708, Bureau of the Budget Enrolled Public Bills, Franklin D. Roosevelt Library.

9. Richard Neustadt, "Presidency and Legislation: The Growth of Central Clearance," *American Political Science Review* 48 (1954): 651. The chronology of the development of central clearance in the Roosevelt administration appears at pp. 647–654.

10. Ibid., pp. 654f. My own examination of the Enrolled Bill file at the Roosevelt Library confirms this fact: The records for bills vetoed prior to that date are very sparse; they are much more complete for vetoes that occurred after that time.

11. Neustadt, "Presidency and Legislation," p. 655.

12. Ibid., pp. 655f.

13. Larry Berman, *The Office of Management and Budget and the Presidency, 1921–1979* (Princeton: Princeton University Press, 1979), p. 13.

14. Ibid., pp. 19f.

15. Stephen Wayne and James F.C. Hyde, Jr., "Presidential Decision-Making on Enrolled Bills," *Presidential Studies Quarterly* 8 (1978): 286.

16. "Presidential Clearance of Legislation," p. 81, Papers of Richard E. Neustadt, Harry S Truman Library.

17. Ibid., p. 82.

18. Ibid., pp. 83f.

19. Wayne and Hyde, "Presidential Decision-Making," p. 286.

20. Letter dated August 28, 1941, from Leon Henderson to the President, OF 47, Veto Message Abstracts, 1940–1945, Franklin D. Roosevelt Library.

# CHAPTER THREE

21. Letter dated February 9, 1944, from Arthur J. Altmeyer
to Judge Samuel J. Rosenman, OF 47, Veto Message Abstracts,
1940–1945, Franklin D. Roosevelt Library.

22. Presidential Memorandum for the Attorney General,
November 29, 1940, OF 47, Veto Message Abstracts, 1940–1945,
Franklin D. Roosevelt Library.

23. Neustadt, "Presidency and Legislation," p. 658.

24. Ibid.

25. Ibid., p. 662.

26. Wayne and Hyde, "Presidential Decision-Making,"
p. 287.

27. Oral History Interview with Roger W. Jones, Washington, D.C., August 14, 1969, p. 39, Harry S Truman Library.

28. Ibid., pp. 53f.

29. Memorandum for Stephen J. Spingarn, "Miscellany on
Executive Office Relationships," June 12, 1950, Papers of Richard E. Neustadt, "Saturday Morning File," Harry S Truman
Library.

30. Wayne and Hyde, "Presidential Decision-Making,"
p. 287, citing an interview with Clark M. Clifford.

31. "The Legislative Clearance Function," Draft of Reports,
1949, p. 7, Papers of Richard E. Neustadt, Harry S Truman
Library.

32. "Extension of the OPA," Budget Bureau Circulars,
1921–1948, Papers of Richard E. Neustadt, Harry S Truman
Library.

33. White House File, Notes on Cabinet Meetings, July 26,
1946, Papers of Matthew J. Connelly, Harry S Truman Library.

34. Ibid., Meeting of June 7, 1946.

35. "Labor-Management Relations Act of 1947," Budget
Bureau Circulars, 1921–1948, Papers of Richard E. Neustadt,
Harry S Truman Library.

36. Papers of Eben A. Ayers, p. 97, Harry S Truman Library.

37. Letter to the President from Thomas C. Buchanan, May
23, 1952, Papers of Harry S Truman, Official File, Harry S
Truman Library.

38. Neustadt, "Presidency and Legislation;" p. 664.

39. Wayne and Hyde, "Presidential Decision-Making,"
p. 287.

40. Bryce Harlow, personal interview; July 20, 1982.
41. Wayne and Hyde, "Presidential Decision-Making," p. 287.
42. Philip Hughes, personal interview, July 22, 1982.
43. Bryce Harlow, personal interview, July 20, 1982.
44. Dwight D. Eisenhower: Papers of President of the United States, 1953–1961, Ann Whitman File, Cabinet Series, Minutes of Cabinet Meeting, February 13, 1956, Dwight D. Eisenhower Library.
45. Minutes of Cabinet Meeting, December 2, 1957, Dwight D. Eisenhower Library.
46. Wayne and Hyde, "Presidential Decision-Making," p. 288
47. Ibid.
48. Letter dated December 23, 1963, to Myer Feldman from William Roth, "Reports on Enrolled Legislation," Container 92, Lyndon B. Johnson Library.
49. Letter dated December 17, 1963, to Myer Feldman from Robert E. Wolf, "Reports on Enrolled Legislation," Container 92, Lyndon B. Johnson Library.
50. Memorandum dated December 23, 1963, for the President from Myer Feldman, "Reports on Enrolled Legislation," Container 92, Lyndon B. Johnson Library.
51. Wayne and Hyde, "Presidential Decision-Making," p. 288.
52. Ibid.
53. Memorandum dated November 3, 1966, for the President from Charles A. Horsky, "Reports on Enrolled Legislation," Container 93, Lyndon B. Johnson Library.
54. Memorandum dated November 10, 1966, for the President from Harry McPherson and Joe Califano, "Reports on Enrolled Legislation," Container 93, Lyndon B. Johnson Library.
55. Charles Schultze, Director of the Bureau of the Budget, personal interview, July 8, 1982.
56. Wayne and Hyde, "Presidential Decision-Making," p. 289.
57. Ibid., p. 290.
58. Wilfred Rommel, personal interview, July 14, 1982.
59. Ibid.
60. Memorandum dated December 28, 1970, for the Presi-

dent from George Shultz, Enrolled Bill File, Office of Management and Budget, Washington, D.C.

61. Memorandum dated June 23, 1971, for the President from George Shultz, ibid.

62. Memorandum dated October 13, 1972, for the President from Caspar Weinberger, ibid.

63. Memorandum dated October 22, 1972, for the President from Caspar Weinberger, ibid.

64. Memorandum dated September 18, 1973, for the President from Roy Ash, ibid.

65. Memorandum dated October 19, 1973, for the President from Roy Ash, ibid.

66. Memorandum undated, for the President from Robert Mayo, Record Group Series, 69.2, Box 297, National Archives, Washington, D.C.

67. Wayne and Hyde, "Presidential Decision-Making," p. 290.

68. Ibid.

69. Memorandum dated August 13, 1974, for the President from Roy Ash, White House Central File, LE-4, Box 4, Gerald R. Ford Library.

70. Memorandum dated April 30, 1975, for Donald Rumsfeld from James T. Lynn, ibid.

71. Alan Moore, Associate Director for Policy and Planning, Domestic Council, personal interview, July 8, 1982.

72. "Domestic Council," Papers of Gerald R. Ford, pp. 3–4, Gerald R. Ford Library.

73. Memorandum dated January 1, 1975, for the President from Ken Cole, White House Records Office: Legislation Case Files, 1974–1976, Box 22, Gerald R. Ford Library.

74. Memorandum dated July 25, 1975, for the President from Jim Cannon, Box 28, Gerald R. Ford Library.

75. Moore, personal interview.

76. Richard Cheney, Chief of Staff, personal interview, July 19, 1982.

77. Moore, personal interview.

78. Wayne and Hyde, "Presidential Decision-Making," p. 291.

79. Cheney, personal interview.

80. James McIntyre, personal interview, July 23, 1982.

81. Memorandum dated November 1978, for the President from James McIntyre, recommending disapproval of a bill that provided for an assistance program for nurses' training. Enrolled Bill File, Office of Management and Budget, Washington, D.C.

82. Memorandum dated October 20, 1978, for the President from James McIntyre, on a bill amending the Small Business Act, ibid.

83. Memorandum dated June 5, 1980, for the President from James McIntyre, on a bill extending the public debt limit and prohibition of a gasoline conservation fee, ibid.

84. McIntyre, personal interview.

85. Memorandum dated September 21, 1978, for the President from James McIntyre, p. 1, White House Central File, Box LE-4, Folder LE-2, 1/1/77–1/20/81, Jimmy Carter Library.

86. Memorandum dated September 21, 1978, for the President from Frank Moore, Stu Eizenstat and Jim McIntyre, White House Central File, Box LE-4, Folder LE-2, 1/1/77–1/20/81, Jimmy Carter Library.

87. Memorandum dated August 16, 1978, for the President from Stu Eizenstat, Domestic Policy Staff, Eizenstat Box 182, Folder, Defense Department 0/A 6217 (1), Jimmy Carter Library.

88. Memorandum dated August 31, 1978, for Hamilton Jordan, Frank Moore, and Dick Moe from Ann Wexler, White House Central File, Box MC-5, Folder MC 3, 8/31/78, Jimmy Carter Library.

89. Memorandum dated August 21, 1978, for the White House Staff from Jerry Rafshoon, White House Central File, Box FI-13, Folder FI 4/F6-13, 7/1/78, Jimmy Carter Library.

90. This information is taken from a document entitled "Legislative Clearance," dated December 1981, which was supplied to me by James Frey, assistant director of OMB for Legislative Reference.

91. Ibid.

92. James Frey, personal interview, June 14, 1982.

93. As indicated in Chapter 2, in recent years, the enrolled bill process has involved 600–700 bills for each two-year Congress.

94. In a few instances, the White House does not request a recommendation from OMB; for example, if a bill is highly

political and the president has already made up his mind regarding the veto, a recommendation is not requested.

95. Stephen J. Wayne, Richard L. Cole, and James F.C. Hyde, Jr., "Advising the President on Enrolled Legislation: Patterns of Executive Influence," *Political Science Quarterly* 94 (1979): 303–317. The analysis, consisting of 238 enrolled bills considered from January 1969 to June 30, 1976, included those for which there was at least one recommendation to veto.

96. As previously indicated in note 10, data on agency recommendations on enrolled bills is particularly limited for early years of the Roosevelt administration. For example, none are available for the first 29 Roosevelt vetoes that occurred in the period from 1933 through 1938. In contrast, of the remaining 230 vetoes included in this study, OMB recommendations were available for 210 of them.

97. John Kennedy actually vetoed a higher percentage of bills favored by the nonlead agencies (33.3%) but that involved only 1 of 3 enrolled bills.

98. Thomas E. Cronin, *The State of the Presidency,* 2d ed. (Boston: Little, Brown and Company, 1980), pp. 276–290.

99. I added to this general category other noncabinet agencies, such as the Council of Economic Advisers, the National Security Council, the Civil Service Commission, and the General Services Administration, which I thought had a similar counseling role to the president and also represented broad interests.

100. Cronin, *State of the Presidency.* I added to this category other noncabinet agencies such as the Federal Security Agency, the Veterans' Administration (which did not acquire cabinet status until 1988), and the Army Corps of Engineers, which I expected to also serve as advocates for their special clientele. I also grouped together agencies with similar functions such as Commerce and Transportation and the Federal Security Agency and Health, Education, and Welfare.

101. The reason that the Veterans' Administration was not involved in a greater number of recommendations was that a considerable number of vetoes of bills affecting veterans occurred in the period 1933 through 1938 (11 in all), when little information on agency recommendations was available from the records.

102. A classic study of the activities and groups supporting the corps is Arthur Maass, *Muddy Water: The Army Engineers and the Nation's Rivers* (Cambridge: Harvard University Press, 1951).

103. An example of such a case was the submission of a draft of a veto message on the Submerged Lands bill that represented the views of both the Justice and Interior departments. Memorandum of May 14, 1952, from Philip B. Perlman, Acting Attorney General, to Charles Murphy of the White House Staff, Papers of Harry S Truman, Official File, Tidelands Oil bill, 1945–July 1946, Harry S Truman Library.

104. Roosevelt sent a handwritten message to the Congress, the first since the administration of Theodore Roosevelt, when typewriters came into general use at the White House. *New York Times,* January 25, 1936.

105. Louisiana Senator Huey Long carried on a one-man filibuster against the president's delivery of the message in that way, but unwittingly broke his five-hour filibuster by temporarily leaving the chamber after demanding a quorum; the Senate then granted permission for Roosevelt to address the joint session. *Washington Post,* May 22, 1935.

106. R. Alton Lee, *Truman and Taft-Hartley: A Question of Mandate* (Lexington: University of Kentucky Press, 1966), p. 99.

107. Nancy Lammers (ed.), *The Washington Lobby,* 4th ed. (Washington, D.C.: Congressional Quarterly, 1982), p. 22.

# 4

## OTHER INFLUENCES ON
## PRESIDENTIAL VETOES

As indicated in the previous chapter, over the years the executive branch developed a structured, systematic process for gathering and assessing information and providing advice to the president on enrolled bills. However, the executive branch did not have exclusive influence on the president's veto decisions. Individuals and groups inside and outside government communicated their concerns to the chief executives. In addition, executive branch personnel who were sensitive to political considerations might well have taken the wishes of these individuals and groups into account when they advised the president on veto decisions. They may also have used others as sources of information and arguments in making their case to the president, as well as allies in the attempt to influence his actions regarding legislation.

This chapter discusses four general non–executive branch groups that became involved in decisions regarding presidential vetoes: (1) members of Congress, (2) state and local officials, (3) political party leaders and campaign officials, and (4) the public.

## MEMBERS OF CONGRESS

Of the many public officials at every level of the American political system who attempted to influence presidential actions in legislation between 1933 and 1981, members of Congress were most intimately involved in such matters on a regular basis. I thus focus first on their activities.

Some of the contacts between the president and members of Congress on pending legislation were designed to *prevent* that legislation from reaching the chief executive's desk for a decision. Franklin Roosevelt sent letters to Vice President Henry Wallace, who also served as president of the Senate, and to Sam Rayburn, speaker of the House of Representatives, asking them to use their influence to stop the enactment of legislation that would have prevented the Commodity Credit Corporation from disposing of its holdings at below-parity prices. The president pointed out, "We cannot afford to indulge in the promotion of selfish interests such as are involved in this legislation."[1]

From the perspective of members of Congress, it was important that they be advised as far ahead of time as possible of the particular action the president was going to take on legislation. President Eisenhower held regular meetings with Republican leaders of Congress to discuss pending bills and legislative strategy. Early in his administration, in response to a query from Republican Representative Samuel McConnell of Pennsylvania on the possibility of a veto of labor legislation amendments, the president said that he looked upon the veto as something to be used only when he felt that "the very foundations of government were being jeopardized." He went on to explain that he felt the machinery of the conferences with the Republican leadership would permit advance notice of positions that would prevent veto situations from developing.[2] However, that hope was not always fulfilled. Senator William Knowland of California, the Republican majority leader, complained that the congressional leadership had not been notified in advance of a veto of a special proposal. White House aide General Wilton Persons conceded that the White House might have done better—that "the committee chairmen and certain other interested parties had been informed but not the leadership."[3]

The Johnson administration also was sensitive to the desirability of providing members of Congress with advance notice of veto decisions. Charles Schultze, director of the Bureau of the Budget, pointed out to Johnson that some indication of administration intentions should be given before a Senate floor vote on a civilian pay bill: "To remain silent during Senate action and *then* to veto the bill would create serious problems."[4]

Although presidents realized that giving members of Congress advance notice of their intentions with respect to legislation was politically wise, at times they regretted such commitments. This was the case in President Truman's handling of the Kerr bill on the regulation of natural gas. He made a commitment to Democratic Senator Robert Kerr of Oklahoma and also to Speaker of the House Sam Rayburn that he would approve the bill but later decided that the bill was not in the public interest. He was particularly concerned about breaking his promise to Rayburn who, unlike Kerr, had no personal financial interest in the bill. One White House aide, Eben Ayers, commented that he had never seen President Truman more troubled over a decision.[5] (The president ended up vetoing the bill.)

Despite the best of intentions, members of Congress and the presidents serving in the 1933–1981 period frequently could not work out difficulties in advance, and it was necessary for the legislators to try to influence presidential decisions at the time a bill was ready for action.

Those who contacted the president to try to influence him *not* to veto a bill provided a variety of reasons for his letting the legislation become law. One was that the bill would benefit some worthy group but not cost the taxpayer much money. Thus, Representative Samuel Pettingill, Democrat of Indiana, wrote to Franklin Roosevelt urging that he sign a bill providing for travel pay during the Philippine Insurrection; he argued that the "men whose fortunes are involved in this bill are few in number, and that the bill, if it becomes law, will make a very small drain on the federal treasury."[6] Or a legislator might indicate the impact that the legislation would have on particular groups and localities. Republican Representative Ulysses Guyer of Kansas submitted a list of states that had troops stationed in the Philippines and that would therefore benefit from a bill providing for the relief of the officers and soldiers of the volunteer service of the United States.[7]

Political considerations were also used as a rationale for the president's signing a bill. Republican Senator Karl Mundt of South Dakota indicated in a meeting of farmstate Republican senators with President Eisenhower regarding a 1958 farm bill that "it was high time that the Republicans gave better evidence that they are in the farmers' corner." He showed the president a poll taken in South Dakota indicating that "Governor Moss, who is running for a congressional seat, is in real trouble." He went on to suggest that "if the Democrats pick up 50 or 60 seats, we will get radical Democrats who will spend us into bankruptcy."[8] Similarly, Republican Senator Homer Capehart of Indiana warned President Eisenhower of the political effects of his vetoing a 1959 housing bill,[9] and Republican Congressman John Rhodes of Arizona urged President Ford to sign the 1974 railroad retirement bill in order to avoid an adverse impact just before the congressional elections.[10] Members of Congress also argued that a veto would prove politically embarrassing to members of the president's party who had strongly supported the bill if they were not properly alerted to a veto possibility: Republican Congressman Charles Halleck of Indiana used that rationale in his unsuccessful attempt to prevent President Eisenhower from vetoing the 1956 natural gas bill.[11]

Finally, some national legislators contacted the president primarily as a means of placating their constituents. During the Johnson administration, Republican Senator Thomas Kuchel of California called the White House regarding a bill for the development of geothermal steam as a power source and said, "I've called; I've done my duty, you do what's best." This statement led presidential aide Harry C. McPherson to conclude, "Clearly he [Kuchel] has no heavy stake in it, but is merely serving some of his constituents."[12]

When presidents decided to veto legislation that members of Congress had urged them to accept, they often tried to justify their actions and to soften the blow for the legislator. FDR wrote to Democratic Senator Claude Pepper of Florida, explaining that he found it necessary to veto a bill dealing with the apportionment of costs for bridges over navigable waters of the United States; he cited veto recommendations from the Federal Works Agency, the War and Treasury departments, and the Bureau of the Budget.[13] Chief executives also referred, as President Eisenhower did, to the veto message as reflecting the reasons for not approving the bill and assured members of Congress (in this case, Republican Congressman Karl LeCompte of Iowa) that despite the decision, his views were carefully considered.[14] Another courtesy that presidents often extended to members of Congress whose views they rejected was to notify them in advance that they were going to veto a bill rather than letting the legislator find out the bad news after the veto had been cast. Dwight Eisenhower informed Democratic Representative Oren Harris of Arkansas that he was vetoing the natural gas bill that Harris had helped steer through Congress.[15] Lyndon Johnson, himself once a powerful senator, took great pains to warn Democratic Senator Carl Hayden of Arizona that he intended to veto a crime bill for the District of Columbia. Presidential aide Harry McPherson remembers that the president insisted that although it was late at night when the veto decision was made that McPherson call Hayden immediately, even if it meant waking him up (which it did). The senator said: "If he can't sign it, he can't. Thanks for calling"—which led McPherson to conclude that "Arizona had known what it was doing for fifty-six years in returning Carl Hayden to Congress."[16]

Members of Congress often urged presidents to sign legislation they favored, and they also tried to influence chief executives to veto bills of which they disapproved. Democratic Congressman Clarence Cannon of Missouri wrote to President Roosevelt expressing his opinion that the vote on the 1937 sugar bill was influenced by a highly organized lobby and suggesting that the president not hesitate to veto the measure.[17] Representatives also urged vetoes of several major pieces of legislation: Republican Representative Robert Michel of Illinois, House minority whip, urged President Ford to veto three major pieces of legislation at the end of the 1975 session—the common situs bill on picketing, a tax measure, and an energy bill.[18]

Along with individual contacts with the White House,

members of Congress also joined forces in attempting to influence presidential decisions on legislation. When Democratic Congressman Samuel Hobbs of Alabama wanted to see President Roosevelt about his general bridge bill, he indicated that he hoped Speaker William Bankhead of Alabama and Majority Leader Sam Rayburn would come with him.[19] Members of state delegations also sought to contact presidents about legislation that was of particular concern to their constituents. A group from Ohio sought to talk to President Roosevelt about a social security bill returning money to that state and also about a bill providing relief for Ohio.[20] Six members of the Wisconsin House delegation wrote to President Eisenhower about a bill that they felt discriminated against the dairy farmers in their state.[21]

Sometimes members of Congress allied along ideological lines in seeking to influence the president. Democratic conservative Senators Harry Byrd of Virginia, Carl Hatch of New Mexico, and Allen Ellender of Louisiana along with conservative Republican Senators Joseph Ball of Minnesota, Robert Taft of Ohio, and Howard Smith of New Jersey, sent a 7,500-word telegram to President Truman in support of the Case labor dispute bill.[22] Liberal Democratic Senators Herbert Lehman of New York, James Murray of Montana, and Estes Kefauver of Tennessee wrote to President Truman urging him to veto the McCarran Internal Security bill.[23]

On occasion a large number of members of Congress worked together to try to influence a president on pending legislation. One hundred thirty-five members of Congress signed a petition urging President Truman to approve the Case bill. A similar number asked him to veto it.[24]

In addition to their interest in whether the president would or should veto a bill, members of Congress also were concerned with the particular wording of veto messages. Democratic Senator Harry Kilgore of West Virginia wrote to President Truman suggesting that five important points be made in the veto message of the 1950 McCarran Internal Security bill, including the appointment of a Presidential Commission on Subversion and Civil Liberties. He went on to explain that "the announcement of such a commission would not only be extremely helpful in securing the votes required to uphold a veto, but it would provide a new and strong basis for the consideration of this type of legislation in the next Congress."[25] During the Carter administration, Republican Representative George Mahon of Texas contacted the White House with suggestions of arguments that should appear in the president's veto message of a 1978 defense appropriations bill.[26] Moreover, executive branch officials recognized the wisdom of seeking the advice of members of Congress on the wording of veto messages. General Frank Hines, head of the Veterans' Administration in the Roosevelt administration, recommended that the advice of leaders of the House and Senate be sought on two 1944 messages dealing with vetoes of legislation affecting veterans of World War I and World War II.[27] Officials were also sensitive to the political effect messages had on members of Congress. When President Ford vetoed a 1974 farm bill, it was suggested that if Secretary of Agriculture Earl Butz planned to increase support levels, mentioning that fact in the veto message would take the "sting" out of the veto for dairy farmers and their representatives.[28]

Members of Congress and presidents also gave consideration to the possibility of an override of a veto when deciding whether a bill should be vetoed. Regular legislative meetings that President Eisenhower had with Republican congressional leaders reflected that concern. At a meeting in early March 1955 at which postal legislation was discussed, Republican Congressman Charles Halleck of Indiana said that he believed that Republican committee members would have great difficulty in sustaining a veto should one occur;[29] later that month Republican Senator William Knowland of California expressed the opinion that the Senate would uphold the president in the event of a veto of the legislation.[30] (The veto was sustained by the Senate on a vote of 54 to 39.)

President Eisenhower expressed differing views on the override issue. He indicated at a 1958 meeting at which a highway bill was discussed that to veto it and have it overridden would be a definite loss of influence. He went on to explain that because he had to veto the rivers and harbor bill, a veto of the highway bill would amount to a total war with Congress; and because the Republican party was not in control of Congress, the veto would be disastrous.[31] However, at a 1959 meeting he told Republican legislative leaders that he was not too concerned if he were overridden in both houses on an airport bill, even though it had much good in it.[32]

Another consideration bearing on the issue of presidential overrides was the scheduling of the veto so that members of Congress could be present when that body received the veto message. This matter came up several times during the Truman administration when major bills were vetoed. Democratic Congressman John Sparkman of Alabama called the White House and requested advance notice as to whether the president planned to veto the Case labor dispute bill, saying that several representatives wished to return to Washington to sustain the president's veto.[33] Republican Senator William Langer of North Dakota phoned to ask when he should be back in Washington so that he could vote on the president's veto of the tidelands oil bill.[34] President Truman also arranged with Speaker Sam Rayburn and Democratic Senator J. Howard McGrath of Rhode Island to send up a veto of a 1950 tax bill at a time when they would be present to lead the vote to sustain the veto.[35]

## STATE AND LOCAL OFFICIALS

Because the United States is a federal system, one might anticipate that in addition to members of Congress, officials at other political levels would become interested in legislation that affected their interests and that they would communicate their concerns to the president or others in the executive branch. This was particularly true of persons serving in state governments in the 1933–1981 period. For example, in 1935, the members of the Iowa Old Age Assistance Commission sent a telegram to President Roosevelt urging him to approve a bill providing financial assistance to veterans of the Spanish-American War. The commissioners contended that the bill "means the keeping of a promise long overdue to these veterans; in addition, it would mean "the circulation of $250,000 in the state of Iowa."[36]

State leaders continued their interest in legislation considered by subsequent presidents. Governor Ellis Arnall of Georgia wrote to President Truman urging him to veto the Reed-Bullwinkle bill, which he said "completely cuts the ground out from under Georgia's anti-trust case against the leading railroads of the nation which is pending in the United States Supreme Court." As the governor saw the situation, "It is not honest, not moral, not fair to change the rules of the game for the benefit of the transportation monopoly in America." Governor Arnall closed the letter with a fervent plea: "So strongly do I believe in you that I am writing you this personal note in the hope that you will measure up to my high appraisal of your character and stamina and my trust in your concern for the average American citizen."[37]

President Truman also received communications from state officials on the highly controversial tidelands oil bill of 1946. Governor Arnall wrote congratulating him for vetoing the bill: "The Congress should not be used as a Cat's Paw to settle judicial questions pending before the Supreme Court of the United States."[38] Other state officials took the opposite position. Governor Earl Warren of California sent Truman a telegram requesting that he sign the bill: "The California legislature in special session again expressed its intense interest in this legislation." The governor argued that "billions of dollars in property rights, both public and private, in our coastal cities, depend upon the establishment of the principle involved in this legislation. These property rights have been considered settled in our state for almost one hundred years, during which period of time the Supreme Court of the United States has uniformly recognized state ownership of Tidelands."[39]

Several officials contacted President Eisenhower on legislation that was of concern to their states. The president wrote to Jacob Javits, attorney general of the state of New York, in 1956, thanking him for his telegram approving the veto of a farm bill. As the president explained: "The fact must be emphasized again and again, as we know, that only those things good for all the United States are good for any major part of it."[40] Two years later President Eisenhower wrote a similar note to Governor George D. Clyde of Utah thanking him for his congratulations for the veto of the farm freeze bill.[41] President

Eisenhower also wrote to Governor Edmund Brown of California concerning the governor's telegram with regard to the veto of a bill dealing with housing. The president explained that he had asked for a revised bill in place of the vetoed one and that the one then before Congress still had some objectionable provisions. He assured the governor that he would carefully consider his comments before taking any action on it.[42]

Contacts with state officials on national legislation continued in more recent presidencies with executive branch officials rather than the president himself frequently handling matters. James Falk, associate director of the Domestic Council, wrote to Governor Hugh Carey of New York saying that President Ford asked him to thank the governor for his letter expressing his objections to the veto of a bill extending health services. He assured Governor Carey that "having the benefit of your opinions on this legislation is extremely helpful, and the President has asked me to pass them along to those on his staff responsible for assisting him in this area."[43] Roland L. Elliott, director of correspondence, replied to a letter to President Ford from the Honorable Connally McKay, associate justice of the Texas Court of Civil Appeals, expressing the president's thanks for the justice's support of "the vetoes he has used in the effort to control the growth of federal spending and to achieve important improvements in several pieces of legislation."[44] A memorandum for Chief of Staff Dick Cheney from White House aide Jerry H. Jones noted that Governor James Holshouser of North Carolina had called, indicating that he thought President Ford should veto the energy bill because the cost controls "are not worth the political costs in Texas and Oklahoma"; that there would be "no big problems with decontrolled prices"; and that "the market system is working to keep prices below FEA [Federal Energy Administration] guidelines." Jones also reported that the governor said that "major oil companies could be persuaded to hold the price lines after a successful veto, which would be helpful."[45]

Executive contact with state officials continued in the Carter administration. White House aide Jack Watson wrote to Roland Fischer of the Colorado River Conservation District saying that he appreciated knowing of his concern with President Carter's veto of a public works bill. He assured Fischer that the veto didn't mean that the president didn't support water resource development but that there were simply too many wasteful projects in the bill.[46] President Carter himself wrote to thank a number of governors for their support of the veto of the bill, including James Exon of Nebraska, Robert Strauss of Oregon, Mike O'Callaghan of Nevada, Ella Grasso of Connecticut, John Carroll of Kentucky, James Hunt of North Carolina, Ed Herschler of Wyoming, Reuben Askew of Florida, Edmund Brown of California, Jerry Apadaca of New Mexico, and John Evans of Idaho.[47]

Most executive contacts in the 1933–1981 period were with state officials, but some involved local officials. A member of a board of police commissioners wrote to Truman White House aide Matthew Connally indicating that in his opinion a veto of the tidelands oil bill in 1946 would "meet with such a hue and cry on behalf of the big cities of the state, Los Angeles, San Francisco, Oakland, Long Beach and San Diego who have hundreds of millions invested in harbor tidelands, that the Republicans will win whatever is left to win in November."[48] The mayor of El Paso, Texas, wrote to President Johnson enclosing a resolution unanimously adopted by the city council of that city, respectfully asking him to look with favor on the passage of a bill dealing with agricultural supports.[49]

During the Carter administration, a deputy appointments secretary wrote a McCreary County, Kentucky, judge to explain that although the president did veto the public works bill the judge wrote about, the president did not object to funding for the South Fork project and would recommend funding for that important one.[50]

During the early presidencies of the 1933–1981 period, party leaders expressed concern with legislation that they felt involved major political problems. On June 19, 1947, President Truman met with a group of Democratic National Committee members and state chairmen and vice chairmen from Alabama, Florida, Georgia, Mississippi, North Carolina, and South Carolina who urged him to sign the Taft-Hartley bill. Truman responded by saying that he had not talked with the Republicans or labor leaders and that he was not going to talk to Democrats about the bill; he would make his own decision on the matter. This prompted a Secret Service man who was present to say, "It's been a long time since there has been a president around here with the guts this man has got."[51]

Similarly, Republican party officials tried to communicate various concerns to President Eisenhower. H. J. Porter, a member of the Republican National Committee from Texas, requested a meeting in 1956 with the president to discuss "gas legislation." When it was suggested that he instead meet with Chief of Staff Sherman Adams, Porter replied that although he would enjoy visiting with the chief of staff, there was no use in his going to Washington unless he could discuss the matters personally with the president.[52] Adams responded that President Eisenhower "wants the recommendations for gas legislation prepared for him by his staff. It is obvious that he cannot listen himself to the various suggestions." Adams invited Porter to "come along up here, and I will be glad to discuss what you have in mind."[53]

Several who wrote to Eisenhower received personal replies. In 1956 Bill Emerson, then a student at Westminster College in Missouri (in 1980 he became a member of Congress), sent the president a resolution passed by the Midwest Federation of Young Republicans urging support for a farm bill; Eisenhower replied regretfully that "after studying every detail of the bill over many long hours and searching my mind and my conscience, I felt that I had no alternative but to veto it. In the short run it would have hurt more farmers than it would have helped. In the long run it would have hurt all farmers."[54] The president also wrote to Admiral Charles W. Styer (Ret.), president of the Los Gatos–Saratoga Republican Assembly, thanking him for its support of his veto of the same bill.[55] Two years later Curtis A. Brewer, a Republican precinct committeeman from LeRoy, Kansas, wrote imploring "Ike" not to veto farm-support legislation: "Ever since you started lowering farm prices five years ago our town and community has been in a depression." He went on: "My income is entirely dependent on several farms I own. Last year I did not get enough income to pay income taxes because of low farm prices."[56] Eisenhower replied to "Curtis": "In the best interests of the American farmer and the American people . . . no course was open to me except to veto the farm freeze legislation." He went on to comment: "I regret, of course, that you personally have had such a difficult time in late years, and I trust that conditions will soon improve for you."[57] Jack Nossman, a member of the

CHAPTER FOUR

Republican State Executive Committee of Texas, wrote to "Ike" requesting his approval of the postal pay bill passed by Congress in 1957; however, as he expressed it, "I trust that you will give this matter due consideration, and whatever your decision may be will meet with my acquiescence."[58] After he vetoed the bill, the president replied: "I appreciate your understanding of the difficulties involved in the postal pay raise bill passed by Congress."[59]

I found no communications from political party officials regarding vetoes in the libraries of presidents who succeeded Eisenhower. During the Johnson administration, a 1967 White House memorandum indicated that the Democratic National Committee could help if it sent out excerpts of the president's veto message of the Government Employees' Life Insurance bill to editorial writers around the country.[60] It should be noted, however, that in this case, the Democratic National Committee was not the source of advice to President Johnson on a presidential veto but rather was being used by him to publicize a veto message that the president had already written. During the Ford administration members of his own personal campaign organization, rather than general party officials, sought to influence presidential vetoes. Senator John Tower, head of Ford's presidential primary campaign in Texas, reportedly threatened to resign his post unless the president vetoed the common situs picketing bill and the energy bill.[61] Archer Nelsen, chairman of the Ford Committee in Minnesota, also requested that the president be advised that he strongly recommended a veto of the common situs picketing bill.[62]

Thus, communications from political officials on presidential vetoes during the 1933–1981 period reflected changes in American politics that occurred during that

120

period of time. Political parties became less important in campaign politics and were increasingly replaced by individuals working in personal campaign organizations.[63]

## THE PUBLIC

People who did not hold public, party, or campaign positions also communicated with presidents on enrolled legislation during the period from 1933 to 1981. In most cases, the opinions were advanced by organized interest groups. However, in some instances, individual citizens acting on their own initiative contacted the president or members of the executive branch on matters of concern to them. Hundreds of communications are on file in presidential libraries. The following discussion focuses on a few important veto decisions and seeks to convey a sense of the groups and individuals who communicated with the president and the type of arguments and opinions they expressed.

A particularly salient issue during the administration of Franklin Roosevelt was that involving veterans' bonuses. Early in his administration, he received a telegram from a World War Veterans' Committee from Mississippi meeting at an all-day session to urge members of that state's congressional delegation to support a bonus for those who served in the military. The telegram stated that Congress had advised their group that the president was opposed to the bill but they did not know the grounds for the objection. The telegram went on, "We are therefore extending to you the courtesy and kindly request that you wire to this meeting any good and valid reasons why adjusted compensation certificates should not be paid immediately."[64] The following year, 1935, a member of an

American Legion post in Conway, Arkansas, requested that President Roosevelt release Senator Joe Robinson from any obligations and allow him to vote his own convictions concerning the bonus bill.[65] Three years later, in 1938, President Roosevelt received a plea from a veteran of the Spanish-American War to sign a bonus bill: "As the adjutant of Colonel Crawford Camp #105 Spanish War Veterans, located in the city of Connellsville, Pennsylvania, I appeal to you on behalf of us veterans and knowing your humanly heart to help us veterans while we are still in this great country of ours as I am at this time affected with high blood pressure, an ulcer in my stomach, and rheumatism."[66]

Although much of the mail received by President Roosevelt on veterans' legislation urged him to sign the measures, his vetoes of them also drew support from some citizens. An attorney in Pittsfield, Massachusetts, said that a veto of the 1934 bonus "set forth the great principle that military service does not in and of itself carry with it the right thereafter to demand special privileges or benefits from the government. I deeply regret that none of our Democratic Representatives from Massachusetts stood by you."[67] Another attorney from Camden, New Jersey, wrote: "I am a Republican and a Hoover man. Nevertheless, I cannot refrain from writing to you through your secretaries that I approve of your veto message to the Congress in regard to the veterans' aid increase. I think that the principles you have discussed in your message are sound and that they should be adhered to. Public clamor should not swerve you from the things you believe to be right."[68] Roosevelt even received a communication from a New York City veteran who supported his veto of the 1934 bonus bill: "As an enrolled Republican voter, a veteran of the recent war, and a former member of the

American Legion, please note that it was a distinct pleasure to read your courageous veto message of veterans' legislation."[69]

Another major focus of public attention during the Roosevelt administration was the Smith-Connally bill of 1943 that prohibited strikes, lockouts, and stoppages of production in certain plants, mines, and facilities involved in the prosecution of the war. Organized labor urged the president to veto the measure. William Green, president of the American Federation of Labor (AFL), Philip Murray, president of the Congress of Industrial Organizations (CIO), and David Robertson, president of the Brotherhood of Locomotive Firemen and Engineers, sent President Roosevelt a detailed analysis of the bill. Calling it, "the worst anti-labor bill passed by Congress in the last hundred years," they warned the president that AFL and CIO representatives might withdraw from the War Labor Board if he signed the anti-strike bill.[70] James Patton, president of the National Farmers' Union, wrote the president, "It is unthinkable that because of the irresponsible action of one man [John L. Lewis] who has withdrawn his pledged word not to strike, all of organized labor is, in practical effect, to be stripped of the freedom to organize and to bargain collectively." He went on to say, "It is time to distinguish between enemies and friends and to fight the enemies. John L. Lewis is an enemy; he is a confessed believer in the dismal doctrines of Hooverism."[71] A wide variety of other local labor organizations from various sections of the country also joined in the effort to convince the president to veto the bill.

However, there were also opposing voices urging President Roosevelt to sign the legislation. Particularly in evidence were people who had families in the armed services. One woman wrote the president, "As a mother of two

R# CHAPTER FOUR

young officers, medical and aviation, now in Africa, I feel
it is my duty to them and to all fighting men overseas as
well, to urge that you sign the Connally anti-strike bill.
No worker has the right to endanger the country's war
efforts and prolong hostilities." [72] Another person with
three sons in the armed services wrote: "We have laws
against murder. But only a fraction of one percent commit
murder. We should have laws to stop racketeers calling
strikes, especially in these times. Hope you sign the Connally Bill that would give us mothers some hope." [73] Another letter from a person in Texas stated, "Speaking for
the citizens of Dawson County with more men in the
armed forces of our country than any other county in
Texas in our population bracket, we take this means to
earnestly urge immediate legislation to curb all types of
labor disputes and strikes for the duration." [74]

Labor legislation drew a great deal of mail from interest groups during the Truman administration. The Case
bill of 1946 that provided for the appointment of fact-
finding boards to investigate labor disputes seriously
affecting the public interest became the occasion for con-
certed interest group activity. Eben Ayers, a White House
aide, said that by Friday, June 7, 1946, "Close to 40,000
telegrams had been received since Truman's radio speech
on the subject on May 24." He suggested, "It has not been
possible to count those for and against the Case bill but it
is apparent that the labor unions had promoted many of
the messages urging a veto, while those urging the president to sign the bill have been more of spontaneous character. Many have come from business people but others
from plain citizens, men and women." [75] Memoranda to
the president summarized some of the arguments. Philip
Murray, president of the CIO, presented a diatribe against
the bill, which he said was sired by "labor haters" who

124

wished to shackle labor; he warned that it would encourage and increase labor disputes and that its proposals are "merely servings from a warmed-over anti-labor stew which has been kept brewing for the past ten years." The president of the Union Labor Life Insurance Company urged the president to veto the Case bill as "ill-founded, ill-designed, and impractical."[76]

However, labor's campaign against the Case bill was nothing compared to its efforts to convince Truman to veto the Taft-Hartley bill. In his detailed account of the battle over the historic piece of legislation, Lee reports that the final total of communications numbered over 750,000.[77] Philip Murray, president of the CIO, wrote to the president urging him to veto the legislation, calling it "the keystone in a program to legislate a new depression" and "a massive governmental assault upon labor unions and an abandonment of collective bargaining."[78] Lee lists a number of other major labor organizations that urged President Truman to veto the legislation, including the American Federation of Musicians, the International Typographical Union, and hundreds of local unions, state labor councils, and smaller national unions. They were joined by the National Catholic Welfare Conference, the National Council of Jewish Women, Americans for Democratic Action, the Union Labor Legionnaires, and the National Farmers' Union. Organizations urging the president to sign the legislation included the American Farm Bureau, the National Grange, and the American Association of Small Businessmen.[79]

The McCarran-Walter bill relating to immigration drew opposing views from concerned groups. Urging that President Truman sign the legislation was the president general of the National Society of Daughters of the American Revolution, who spoke on behalf of the 170,000 members of the organization.[80] Joining in the support of the bill was the chairman of the Pacific Southwest District Council of the Japanese-American Citizens' League, who stated that the bill "includes provisions for the elimination of racial restrictions in our immigration and naturalization laws, restrictions that have branded and stigmatized persons of Japanese ancestry as both undesirable and not good enough for American citizenship."[81] Those who tried to persuade President Truman to veto the bill included the secretary of the National Conference of Catholic Charities, who stated that "the McCarran bill is a negation of the Christian ideals of immigration that have been promoted by Our Most Holy Father, Pius XII,"[82] and the chairman of the Brownsville, Texas, Citizens' Committee of 1000 for Justice in the case of Henry Fields, Jr., who argued, "This bill would virtually eliminate immigration from the West Indies, which consists mainly of Negro people."[83]

## NOTES

1. Memorandum dated February 24, 1942, from President Roosevelt to Leon Henderson, Administrator, Office of Price Administration, OF 419-D, Pending Legislation, 1942–1945, Franklin D. Roosevelt Library.

2. Legislative meeting of March 9, 1953, Ann Whitman File, Legislative Meetings, 1953–1961 Box, Dwight D. Eisenhower Library.

3. Legislative meeting of February 15, 1954, ibid.

4. Memorandum dated June 20, 1966, for the President from Charles Schultze, Legislation (EX-LE/PE), Container 148, Lyndon B. Johnson Library.

5. Papers of Eben A. Ayers, 1950 Folder, p. 52, Harry S Truman Library.

6. Letter dated August 30, 1935, to President Franklin Roosevelt, OF 45a, Box 1, Spanish-American War Veterans, 1933–1935, Franklin D. Roosevelt Library.

7. Letter of August 20, 1935, to President Roosevelt, OF 47, Veto Message Abstracts, 1933–1935, Franklin D. Roosevelt Library.

8. Memorandum for Mrs. Ann Whitman, dated March 28, 1958, from Jack Z. Anderson, D.D.E. Diary Series, Staff Notes 58(1), Box 31, Dwight D. Eisenhower Library.

9. Memorandum dated June 30, 1959, for General Wilton Persons from Robert Merriam, Central Files, OF 120, 1959 (2), Dwight D. Eisenhower Library.

10. Memorandum dated October 11, 1974, to President Ford from John D. Marsh, Jr., White House Central Files, Case File on HR 115301, Box 9, Gerald R. Ford Library.

11. Memorandum dated February 13, 1956, from Charles Halleck to Sherman Adams, Wilton B. Persons, and Gerald D. Morgan, Gerald Morgan Papers, Box 20, Natural Gas #3, Dwight D. Eisenhower Library.

12. Memorandum dated November 8, 1966, for President Johnson from Harry C. McPherson, Jr., "Reports on Enrolled Legislation," Box 93, Lyndon B. Johnson Library.

13. Presidential Memorandum dated June 8, 1940, to Senator Pepper, OF 47, Veto Message Abstracts, 1940–1945, Franklin D. Roosevelt Library.

14. Letter dated April 16, 1956, from Dwight Eisenhower to Republican Congressman Karl M. LeCompte of Iowa, OF 106-K, Box 506, Dwight D. Eisenhower Library.

15. Letter dated February 23, 1956, from Dwight Eisenhower to the Honorable Oren Harris, OF 140-C, Box 726, Dwight D. Eisenhower Library.

16. Harry C. McPherson, A Political Education (Boston: Atlantic Monthly Press, 1972), pp. 280f.

17. Letter dated August 7, 1937, from Representative Cannon to President Roosevelt, OF 47, Veto Message Statements, 1936–1939, Franklin D. Roosevelt Library.

18. Letter dated December 10, 1975, from Congressman Michel to President Ford, White House Central File, LE 11/12/75-12/31/75, Gerald R. Ford Library.

19. Memorandum dated March 29, 1940, for President Roo-

CHAPTER FOUR

sevelt from General Edwin Watson, PPF 474, Sam Rayburn Folder, Franklin D. Roosevelt Library.

20. Memorandum dated January 23, 1940, from James Rowe for General Watson and Rudolph Forster, OF 47, Veto Messages, 1940–1945, Franklin D. Roosevelt Library.

21. Letter dated April 15, 1956, to President Eisenhower from Congressmen Glenn Davis, John Byrnes, Gardner Withrow, Melvin Laird, Lawrence Smith, and William VanPelt, OF 106-K, Box 506, Farm Bill, Dwight D. Eisenhower Library.

22. *New York Times,* June 7, 1946.

23. Letter dated September 20, 1950, Papers of Harry S Truman, Official File 2750C, Internal Security Legislation, Harry S Truman Library.

24. *New York Times,* June 7, 1946.

25. Letter dated September 14, 1950, Papers of Harry S Truman, Official File 2750C, Internal Security Legislation, Harry S Truman Library.

26. Note dated August 16, 1978, to "Star" from "Joanne," D.P.S. Eizenstat Box 182, Folder, Defense Department of O/A 6127 (1), Jimmy Carter Library.

27. Memorandum dated May 26, 1944, for President Roosevelt from General Edwin Watson, OF 47, Veto Message Abstracts, 1940–1945, Franklin D. Roosevelt Library.

28. Memorandum dated December 30, 1974, for Warren Hendriks from Vern Loew, White House Records Office, Box 22, Enrolled Bill File on S 4206, Gerald R. Ford Library.

29. Memorandum dated March 1, 1955, for Director Philip Hughes from L. A. Minnich, Jr., Ann Whitman File, Legislative Meetings, 1955, Box 1, Folder 2, Dwight D. Eisenhower Library.

30. Memorandum dated March 22, 1955, for Director Hughes from L. A. Minnich, Jr., Dwight D. Eisenhower Library.

31. Entry of April 16, 1958, D.D.E. Diaries, Telephone Calls, April 1958, Dwight D. Eisenhower Library.

32. Legislative meeting of June 16, 1959, Ann Whitman File, Box 3 (1959), Folder 5, Dwight D. Eisenhower Library.

33. Memorandum dated May 29, 1946, from M.J.C. (Matthew Connally) for the President, White House Official File, Harry S Truman Library.

34. Memorandum dated May 21, 1952, for Charles Murphy, White House Official File, Harry S Truman Library.

35. Memorandum dated April 2, 1978, for the File on Veto of Tax Bill, H.R. 4970. Elsey Papers, Legis. 80th Cong., 2d sess., Harry S Truman Library.

36. Telegram dated August 29, 1935, to the White House from John F. Porterfield, Mrs. E. R. Meredith, Byron G. Allen, and A. L. Urick, OF 45–45a, Box 1, Spanish-American War Veterans, 1933–1945, Franklin D. Roosevelt Library.

37. Letter dated June 1, 1948, from Ellis Arnall, Governor of Georgia, to President Truman, Papers of Harry S Truman, Official File 277, August 1946–1948, Harry S Truman Library.

38. Telegram dated August 5, 1946, from Governor Arnall to President Truman, Papers of Harry S Truman, Official File 56F, August 1946–1948, Box 273, Harry S Truman Library.

39. Telegram dated July 26, 1946, from Governor Warren to President Truman, Papers of Harry S Truman, Official File 56F, 1945–July 1946, Harry S Truman Library.

40. Letter dated April 19, 1956, to Attorney General Javits from President Eisenhower, Official File 106-K, Box 506, Dwight D. Eisenhower Library.

41. Letter dated April 3, 1958, to Governor Clyde from President Eisenhower, Official File 106-H, Box 502, Dwight D. Eisenhower Library.

42. Letter dated September 11, 1959, to Governor Brown from President Eisenhower, Official File 120, Box 616, Dwight D. Eisenhower Library.

43. Letter dated January 28, 1975, from Director Falk to Governor Carey, White House Central File LE-4, Box 4, Gerald R. Ford Library.

44. Letter dated August 29, 1975, from Director Elliot to Justice McKay, White House Central File LE-4, Box 5, Gerald R. Ford Library.

45. Memorandum dated December 4, 1975, from Mr. Jones to Mr. Cheney, White House Central File U1, Box 5, Gerald R. Ford Library.

46. Letter to Mr. Fischer from Mr. Watson, White House Central File, Box LE-4, Folder LE-2 (1-20-77 to 1-20-81), Jimmy Carter Library.

47. Letter from President Carter to named governors, Box LE-4, Folder LE-2 (9-1-78 to 1-20-78), Jimmy Carter Library.

48. Letter dated August 1, 1946, from Al Colvin to "Matt,"

Papers of Harry S Truman, Official File 56F, August 1946–1948, Harry S Truman Library.

49. Letter dated August 9, 1968, from Judson F. Williams to President Johnson, White House Central Files, LE/TAG/COTTON, Container 15, Lyndon B. Johnson Library.

50. Letter dated November 8, 1978, to Jimmy W. Green from Fran Vordes, White House Central File, Box LE-4, Folder LE-2 (9-1-78 to 1-20-81), Jimmy Carter Library.

51. Papers of Eben A. Ayers, Diary entry of June 19, 1947, Harry S Truman Library.

52. Letter dated March 26, 1956, from Porter to Governor Adams, Official File 140-C, Box 726, Dwight D. Eisenhower Library.

53. Letter dated March 28, 1956, from Adams, Official File 140-C, Box 726, Dwight D. Eisenhower Library.

54. Letter dated April 19, 1956, from President Eisenhower, Official File 106-K, Box 506, Dwight D. Eisenhower Library.

55. Letter dated April 23, 1956, from President Eisenhower, Official File 106-K, Box 506, Dwight D. Eisenhower Library.

56. Letter dated March 24, 1958, from Brewer to President Eisenhower, Official File 106-H, Box 502, Dwight D. Eisenhower Library.

57. Letter dated March 31, 1958, from President Eisenhower, Official File 106-H, Box 502, Dwight D. Eisenhower Library.

58. Letter dated August 28, 1957, from Nossman to President Eisenhower, Official File 104-N-7, Box 484, Dwight D. Eisenhower Library.

59. Letter dated September 5, 1957, from President Eisenhower, Official File 104-N-7, Box 484, Dwight D. Eisenhower Library.

60. Memorandum dated August 15, 1967, to "Marvin" from "Fred," Executive File (LE/1S 5-1), Legislative Container 76, Lyndon B. Johnson Library.

61. *Dallas Morning News,* November 26, 1975. A memorandum of that date to the president from Max L. Friedersdorf indicated that the newspaper clipping had been picked up by the staff in Texas Republican Representative Allan Steelman's office. White House Central File, LA 6, Box 8, Gerald R. Ford Library.

62. Memorandum dated December 6, 1975, to the President from Max L. Friedersdorf, White House Central File, LA 6, Box 8, Gerald R. Ford Library.

63. William Crotty, *American Parties in Decline* 2d ed. (Boston: Little, Brown and Company, 1984), represents that point of view, which is shared by many other political scientists. For a contrary opinion, see Larry J. Sabato, *The Party's Just Begun* (Glenville, Ill.: Scott, Foresman and Company, 1988).

64. Telegram dated March 1, 1934, to the President from Mississippi War Veterans' Committee, OF 95c, Box 3, Soldiers' Bonus Folder, 1934, Franklin D. Roosevelt Library.

65. Communication dated April 26, 1935, to the President from Jesse W. Grisham, OF 95c, Soldiers' Bonus Folder, 1935, Franklin D. Roosevelt Library.

66. Letter dated May 5, 1938, to the President from Jesse Murphy, OF 45a, Box 1, Soldiers' Bonus Folder, 1936-1938, Franklin D. Roosevelt Library.

67. Letter dated March 28, 1934, to the President from James M. Rosenthal, OF 95c, Box 4, Soldiers' Bonus Folder, 1934, Franklin D. Roosevelt Library.

68. Letter dated March 28, 1934, to the President from Lawrence N. Peck, OF 45a, Box 1, Soldier's Bonus Folder, 1936–1938, Franklin D. Roosevelt Library.

69. Letter dated March 29, 1934, to the President from John A. Lyon, OF 95c, Box 4, Soldiers' Bonus Folder, Franklin D. Roosevelt Library.

70. *Washington Post,* June 18, 1943.

71. Letter dated June 19, 1943, to the President from Mr. Patton, PPF 474, Folder 474, Franklin D. Roosevelt Library.

72. Letter dated June 19, 1943, to the President from Alma S. Benzing, OF 407b, Box 14, Franklin D. Roosevelt Library.

73. Telegram dated June 21, 1943, to the President from Mabel Sexton, OF 407b, Box 14, Franklin D. Roosevelt Library.

74. Letter dated June 19, 1943, to the President from Kilmer B. Corbin, OF 407b, Box 14, Franklin D. Roosevelt Library.

75. Papers of Eben A. Ayers, 1946 Folder, Harry S Truman Library.

76. Papers of George Elsey, Labor Legislation, Harry S Truman Library.

# CHAPTER FOUR

77. R. Alton Lee, *Truman and Taft-Hartley: A Question of Mandate* (Lexington: University of Kentucky Press, 1966), p. 81, citing a memorandum dated September 9, 1949, from William D. Hassett to Secretary of Labor Maurice Tobin, Truman Papers, OF 15, Harry S Truman Library.

78. Papers of Robert A. Taft, Sr., Container 677, Legislative File, Labor Legislation 1947, Folder 1, Manuscript Division, Library of Congress.

79. Lee, *Truman and Taft-Hartley,* pp. 83–86.

80. Letter dated May 29, 1952, from Mrs. James B. Patton to the President, OF 133 HR 2678, "Pro," Harry S Truman Library.

81. Letter dated May 29, 1952, from Tut Yata to the President, OF 133 HR 2678, "Pro," Harry S Truman Library.

82. Letter dated May 26, 1952, to the President, OF 133 HR 2678, "Con," Harry S Truman Library.

83. Letter dated February 6, 1952, from Bishop Reginald G. Barrow to the President, OF 133 HR 2678, "Con," Harry S Truman Library.

# 5

# REASONS FOR AND
# PUBLIC-POLICY EFFECTS
# OF PRESIDENTIAL VETOES

In this chapter I shift from an examination of the *dynamics* of the process by which decisions are made on presidential vetoes to the *results* of that process. The first two sections focus on the reasons presidents veto legislation. The third analyzes the effect that presidential vetoes have on national policy-making.

## THE FOUNDERS' VIEWS OF REASONS
## FOR PRESIDENTIAL VETOES

As indicated in Chapter 1, the Founders differed not only on the form that the presidential veto should take but also on the reasons for vesting the veto power in the president. They suggested a variety of reasons for placing that power in the chief executive. Madison in particular articulated his views on the matter during the deliberations of the Constitutional Convention. At one point in the proceedings,[1] he suggested that an executive veto would serve three distinct purposes. It would be useful to the *executive* "by inspiring additional confidence and firmness" in exerting what he termed the "revisionary" power. It would be useful for the *legislature* because of "the valuable assistance it would give in preserving a consistency, conciseness, perspicacity, and technical propriety in the laws, qualities particularly necessary and yet shamefully wanting in our Republic Code." Finally, it would be useful to the *community at large* "as an additional check against a pursuit of those unwise and unjust measures which constituted so great a portion of our calamities." Later in the deliberations he expressed similar views on the purposes of the veto: It was to "defend the executive's rights and to prevent popular or factional injustice";[2] it was also meant "as a check to precipitate, to unjust and to unconstitutional laws."[3]

The rationale for the veto also was made at state conventions called to ratify the Constitution. James Wilson, one of the major framers of the Constitution, expressed the sentiment at the Pennsylvania convention that the president would benefit from special advantages in policy-making; as "the man of the people," the president would have the fullest information about the nation's situation, including access to foreign and domestic records and communications, as well as advice from executive officers in different departments of the general government.[4]

Still another major source of information about the Founders' intentions with respect to the president's veto power is *Federalist 73*, generally ascribed to Alexander Hamilton. His views parallel those of Madison. "It not only serves as a shield to the Executive but it also furnishes additional security against the enaction of improper laws."[5] Hamilton explains: "It establishes a salutary check on the legislative body, calculated to guard against the effects of faction, precipitancy, or any impulse unfriendly to the public good, which may happen to influence a majority of that body."[6]

Thus, the Founders expressed a number of reasons for granting the president the power to veto legislation passed by Congress. However, it remained for the chief executives themselves to determine the use to which the power would be put and the reasons for utilizing it. As we have noted, the early presidents tended to emphasize constitutional objections, but ultimately what Joseph Kallenbach characterizes as Jackson's "tribunative" view of the veto power prevailed.[7] Writing at the end of the first century of the nation's existence, Edward Mason suggests that the Founders primarily viewed the veto power as a means of preventing unconstitutional encroachments of the legislature upon the executive. However, he concludes that most of the unconstitutional encroachments spelled out in veto messages did not involve the executive branch.[8] Moreover, he states that most vetoes were based on what he terms "expediency." He summarizes the major difference between the veto in 1789 and 1889: "Then it was used sparingly and in a cumbrous manner as a weapon of constitutional warfare; today it is used frequently and easily as a means of preventing mistakes in the administration of the business of government."[9]

The debate over the intentions of the Founders with respect to the veto has continued in recent years. Charles Black, Jr., contends that the "prime original purpose for the inclusion of the power was that it was thought to give the President the means of protecting his own office from Congressional encroachment."[10] He also states less confidently, "There may have been anticipation that it would be used to vindicate the President's own Constitutional views by being interposed against legislation he considered unconstitutional."[11] Professor Black asserts, "What is really proved I think is that *we* have departed in our expectations and in our toleration of presidential practice from the rather clearly demonstrated expectations of those whose expectations count most, the people who presumably knew the Constitution's beginnings."[12]

Louis Fisher takes issue with Black's contention. He argues that Madison viewed the veto power "in more generous terms," pointing to his concern with protecting the rights of the people at large and with preventing the passage of unwise laws or those incorrect in form.[13]

My own view is that Fisher is clearly right on this issue. As indicated above, Madison, Hamilton, and Wilson all enunciated other reasons for the veto power than legislative encroachment on the executive or even than protection against unconstitutional measures of any kind. All three were concerned with preventing what they viewed as unwise, unjust, or improper legislation.

This historical information is helpful in gaining some understanding of reasons presidents should or did veto legislation; I would, however, like to go further and provide a systematic analysis of veto messages over time, particularly in recent years. In addition, I wish to explore the specific reasons presidents gave for vetoing laws they considered unwise. Finally, I will look for reasons presidents gave for vetoing legislation that were not specifically mentioned by the Framers of the Constitution. The following section provides this additional information.

ANALYSIS OF PRESIDENTIAL VETOES, 1933–1981

I began with the basic unit of the 259 vetoes of nationally significant legislation discussed in Chapter 2. However, I also decided to distinguish between regular vetoes and pocket vetoes—ones that Congress has no opportunity to override. For a regular veto, presidents are required by the Constitution to return the vetoed bill to the house in which it originated, setting forth their reasons for not approving it in an official veto message. For a pocket veto presidents can issue a memorandum of disapproval setting forth their objections, but they are not required to. I was concerned that presidents might not have been uniform in their use of memoranda of disapproval and that the nature of the informal memoranda might be different from that of official veto messages. Therefore only the latter were analyzed; they total 169.

Once I determined which veto messages to examine, it was necessary to develop some means of classifying the reasons spelled out in those messages. In the process, a variety of sources was examined: (1) documents containing reasons enunciated by the Framers; (2) a series of studies that attempted to classify reasons given by governors for vetoing state legislation;[14] (3) a number of presidential veto messages. An attempt was made to develop a list that would be all-inclusive and at the same time would delineate the various reasons from each other. After experimenting, I devised five general categories of reasons presidents veto legislation.

1. *Protection of the executive against legislative encroachment*

   Objections based on an improper legislative encroachment on the executive through such devices as legislative vetoes that require the president or other executive officials to obtain the approval of one or both houses of Congress or of certain committees before acting on a matter. Also legislation, for example, that forbids the president or the attorney general from seeking a particular remedy in a federal court.

2. *Unconstitutionality*
   Objections that specifically state that the legislation is unconstitutional because it violates the separation of powers or the division of powers or
   infringes on the rights of individuals or groups.
3. *Administratively unworkable*
   Objections that the meaning of the legislation is
   not clear and hence difficult to administer, that it
   centralizes authority too much, places responsibility in the wrong agency, unnecessarily creates a
   new agency, or wastes government time and effort.
4. *Fiscally unsound*
   Objections that the legislation exceeds the president's budget, expands obligations without providing additional revenues, is inflationary, is not
   needed at the present time, or wastes money.
5. *Unwise Policy*
   Objections included in this category are many
   and varied and will be subsequently analyzed
   in detail.

This classification scheme also involved subjective
judgments. However, it seemed to raise few problems
when it was used to analyze the 169 veto messages. It was
gratifying to find later that it closely parallels one recently referred to by Roger Davidson and also has some
similarity to another developed by Albert Ringelstein.[15]
A final decision to be made in analyzing the reasons
presidents disapprove legislation was whether to select
only the most important reason given for a specific veto or
to take into account additional reasons if such appeared
in the message veto. The relative importance of multiple
reasons was weighted on the basis of where each appeared
in the message and how much space was devoted to each.

Most messages contained more than one reason, but very few involved as many as three reasons. Therefore, I decided to restrict judgments on multi-reason messages to the first and second most important reasons for a given veto.

Table 5.1 shows the relative importance of the five reasons as reflected in the messages associated with regular presidential vetoes from 1933 to 1981. The clearly dominant reason was that the legislation constituted unwise public policy. Two of the reasons stressed by the Framers, the encroachment of the legislature on the executive branch and the unconstitutional nature of the legislation, were relatively infrequent in the veto messages. The remaining two general objections, that the legislation was fiscally unsound and that it was administratively unworkable, were not specifically mentioned by the Framers. The former was second in importance to unwise public policy while the latter was relatively unimportant, ranking about the same as the encroachment and unconstitutional objections.

An analysis of the relationship among the objections

TABLE 5.1. Reasons for Presidential Regular Vetoes, 1933–1981

| Type of Reason | First Reason | | Second Reason[a] | | Total | |
|---|---|---|---|---|---|---|
| | N | % | N | % | N | % |
| Encroachment | 6 | 3.6 | 10 | 8.8 | 16 | 5.6 |
| Unconstitutional | 10 | 5.9 | 8 | 7.0 | 18 | 6.4 |
| Administratively unworkable | 9 | 5.3 | 15 | 13.2 | 24 | 8.5 |
| Fiscally unsound | 33 | 19.5 | 52 | 45.6 | 85 | 30.0 |
| Unwise public policy | 111 | 65.7 | 29 | 25.4 | 140 | 49.5 |
| Total | 169 | 100.0 | 114 | 100.0 | 283 | 100.0 |

[a]In 55 of the 169 messages, only one reason was given for the president's veto.

indicated that some were linked. In 70 messages unwise public policy was the first of two objections noted; in 50 of those messages, the second reason was that the legislation was fiscally unsound. The reverse was also true. In 23 messages, fiscal unsoundness was the first of two reasons cited, and in each of those instances the second objection was that the legislation constituted unwise public policy. Two other reasons that were associated were that the legislation encroached on the executive and that it was unconstitutional. The other objection, that the legislation was administratively unworkable, was most often linked with unwise public policy. These relationships appear to be logical: presidents view legislation that they do not regard as good public policy to be costly and administratively unworkable; that which encroaches on the executive branch is also often thought to be unconstitutional.

With the general pattern of presidential objections in mind, I analyzed the vetoes of the eight presidents according to which of the five reasons was the major one for disapproving legislation. The presidents were also grouped by party to determine whether that factor made any difference in their choice of objections. It was expected, for example, that Republican presidents would be more inclined than Democratic ones to give fiscal unsoundness or administrative unworkability as the reason for vetoing legislation.

Table 5.2 shows that unwise public policy was the most prevalent reason given by all the presidents analyzed, with Democratic presidents somewhat more inclined than Republican ones to give that characteristic as the main reason for vetoing legislation. As expected, the Republican chief executives, led by Richard Nixon, were generally more likely than Democratic ones to make fiscal unsoundness the most important objection to legis-

TABLE 5.2. Most Important Reason Given by Various Presidents for Vetoing Legislation, 1933–1981 (in percent)

| President | Unwise Policy | Fiscally Unsound | Admin. Unworkable | Uncons. | Encroach. | Total |
|---|---|---|---|---|---|---|
| *Republican* | | | | | | |
| Eisenhower | 65.0 | 30.0 | 5.0 | | | 20 |
| Nixon | 45.8 | 41.7 | | 12.5 | | 24 |
| Ford | 69.0 | 16.7 | 2.4 | 7.1 | 4.8 | <u>42</u> |
| Overall | 61.6 | 26.7 | 2.3 | 7.0 | 2.3 | 86 |
| | | | | | | |
| *Democratic* | | | | | | |
| Roosevelt | 76.3 | 15.8 | 2.6 | 5.3 | | 38 |
| Truman | 73.3 | 3.3 | 20.0 | 3.3 | | 30 |
| Kennedy | | | | | | |
| Johnson | | 50.0 | | | 50.0 | 4 |
| Carter | 63.6 | 9.1 | | 9.1 | 18.2 | <u>11</u> |
| Overall | 69.9 | 12.0 | 8.4 | 4.8 | 4.8 | 83 |
| | | | | | | |
| Total | | | | | | 169 |

lation. However, administrative unworkability was not more favored by Republican presidents than Democratic ones. In fact, that objection was used most by Harry Truman. It should be noted, however, that it appeared as the major reason in a total of only 9 of the 169 messages analyzed, with Truman identified with 6 of them.

Another matter I explored was whether the types of general public policy areas discussed in Chapter 2 were significant in the major reason given for vetoing legislation. Table 5.3 indicates that unwise public policy was the major reason given by presidents for vetoing all four general types of public policy. The fiscally unsound objection was associated most often with social welfare legislaion and legislation involving government management.

TABLE 5.3. Most Important Reason for Vetoing Legislation by General Policy Area, 1933–1981 (in percent)

| General Policy Area[a] | Type of Reason | | | | | |
|---|---|---|---|---|---|---|
| | Unwise Policy | Fiscally Unsound | Admin. Unwkable | Unconst. | Encroach. | Total |
| Civil liberty and rights | 57.1 | | 28.6 | 14.3 | | 7 |
| International involvement | 65.2 | 8.7 | 4.4 | 8.7 | 13.0 | 23 |
| Social welfare | 69.1 | 25.0 | 2.9 | 2.9 | | 68 |
| Gov't management | 63.6 | 18.2 | 6.1 | 7.6 | 4.5 | 66 |
| Total | | | | | | 164 |

[a]It was impossible to classify five of the vetoes that were associated with general appropriation bills.

Administrative unworkability and unconstitutionality tended to be linked most closely with legislation involving civil liberties and civil rights; encroachment was most associated with bills relating to international involvement. These associations are logical and might be expected, given the nature of the general policy areas analyzed.

The final part of the analysis seeks to define more specifically the types of reasons subsumed under the category of unwise public policy, the general objection registered most often in veto messages. This proved to be the most difficult type of classification.[16] The general categories that were developed are:

1. *Unfair treatment of groups and interests*
   Objections that the legislation unfairly favors or disadvantages a special group or interest, including state and local ones.

2. *Relation to existing policy*
The legislation departs from present policy, duplicates it, or is against settled principles and priorities.

3. *Would set a dangerous precedent*
The emphasis is not so much on the immediate effect of the legislation but that it will open the door to further abuses.

4. *Will not accomplish the purposes the legislation is designed to meet*
The expressed purpose of the legislation cannot be accomplished by the legislation, and it may also bring about unintended, unfavorable consequences.

5. *Against the national interest, the public interest, or basic institutions*
A residual category when none of the above more specific reasons is in the veto message.

6. *Improper method of enactment*
Objections based not on the substance of the legislation but on the conditions under which it was enacted into law.

Table 5.4 indicates that unfair treatment of groups and interests is by far the most prevalent reason within the general objection of unwise public policy, constituting over one-half of all reasons cited. Within that general category, the most frequently cited reason is that the legislation *favors* a special group or interest (as contrasted to *disadvantaging* such a group or interest); 35.7 percent of all reasons cited are on that basis alone. The remaining reasons for vetoing the legislation as unwise public policy are of the same general frequency, with the exception of improper method of enactment, which represents only about 1 percent of all specific reasons cited.

# CHAPTER FIVE

TABLE 5.4. Specific Reasons Given in Veto Messages Stressing the General Category of Unwise Public Policy, 1933–1981

|  | Number[a] | Percent |
|---|---|---|
| Unfair treatment of groups or interests | 73 | 52.1 |
| Relation to present policy | 17 | 12.1 |
| Would set a dangerous precedent | 10 | 7.1 |
| Would not accomplish purpose | 22 | 15.7 |
| Not in national or public interest | 16 | 11.4 |
| Improper method of enactment | 2 | 1.4 |
| Total | 140 | 99.8[b] |

[a]There were 29 veto messages in which unwise public policy was not mentioned as a reason for the president's disapproving the legislation.
[b]Total does not add to 100% owing to rounding.

A comparison of the frequency with which individual presidents referred to unfair treatment of groups or interests in their veto messages stressing unwise public policy showed that Franklin Roosevelt cited it most often (70.6 percent). Among general policy areas it was most prevalent in legislation involving social welfare legislation (57.1 percent). Within that general category, the specific policy area with which it was most often associated was veterans' legislation (77.8 percent).

One final point should be noted. The reasons presidents give in veto messages for disapproving legislation represent only one type of objection—that which can be openly admitted and which is considered to be justifiable. (That type of objection is generally provided by executive agencies described in Chapter 3.) However, presidents also veto legislation for political reasons as well. For example, President Truman's 1947 veto of the Taft-Hartley bill is sometimes ascribed to his desire to win favor with organized labor and thereby to counteract Henry Wallace's possible third-party bid for the presidency in 1948.[17]

# REASONS FOR AND EFFECTS OF VETOES

## PUBLIC-POLICY EFFECTS OF PRESIDENTIAL VETOES

When a president casts a regular veto—not a pocket veto—he returns the affected bill to the house in which it originated—the Senate or the House of Representatives. As discussed earlier, he also issues an official veto message setting forth his reasons for exercising the veto. The chamber involved must then decide what to do about the matter. It may take an immediate vote to sustain or override the veto, or the vote may be postponed to a fixed date. If the congressional party leaders calculate that they do not have the necessary two-thirds votes to override the president's veto, the matter may be referred to a committee, and if it is not reported back to the entire chamber—which is typically the case—the veto is considered to be unchallenged. A vote to sustain the president's veto or not to challenge it ends the matter. If the chamber decides by a two-thirds vote to override the president's veto, the bill is sent to the second chamber, which has similar options in dealing with it. Only if the second house also votes to override the bill by a two-thirds vote is the veto overridden by the entire Congress; the bill thus becomes law.

Table 5.5 indicates that Congress often did override Presidents Roosevelt through Carter on nationally significant legislation. As indicated by the final column on the right, 24 percent of the regular vetoes were ultimately overridden by Congress. Column 4 shows that Congress attempted to override presidential vetoes 62 percent of the time when it could do so, and 39 percent of those attempts were successful (see column 6).

The table also shows great variation in the way in which Congress responded to vetoes cast by the various presidents. President Truman was ultimately overridden the greatest percentage of the time, 37; however, Congress

# CHAPTER FIVE

TABLE 5.5. Congressional Response to Regular Vetoes of
Nationally Significant Legislation, 1933–1981

| President | Vetoes | Override Attempts No. | Override Attempts % | Successful Overrides No. | Successful Overrides % | Vetoes Overridden (Percentages) |
|---|---|---|---|---|---|---|
| Roosevelt | 38 | 19 | 50.0 | 9 | 47.4 | 23.7 |
| Truman | 30 | 22 | 73.3 | 11 | 50.0 | 36.7 |
| Eisenhower | 20 | 10 | 50.0 | 2 | 20.0 | 10.0 |
| Kennedy | 0 | 0 | 0.0 | 0 | 0.0 | 0.0 |
| Johnson | 4 | 0 | 0.0 | 0 | 0.0 | 0.0 |
| Nixon[a] | 24 | 21 | 87.5 | 5 | 23.8 | 20.8 |
| Ford | 42 | 28 | 66.7 | 12 | 42.9 | 28.6 |
| Carter | 11 | 4 | 36.4 | 2 | 50.0 | 18.2 |
| Total | 169 | 104 | 61.5 | 41 | 39.4 | 24.3 |

SOURCES: *Presidential Vetoes,* 1789–1976 comp. Senate Library (Washington, D.C.: Government Printing Office, 1978); *Presidential Vetoes,* 1977–1984 comp. Senate Library (Washington, D.C.: Government Printing Office, 1985).

[a]Does not include action on 2 pocket vetoes that were later declared to be unconstitutional.

attempted to override President Nixon more than any other president—on 87 percent of his vetoes. Presidents Truman and Carter share the dubious distinction of being successfully overridden by Congress on the greatest proportion of attempts—50 percent.

The overrides of President Truman's vetoes also occurred on the most important bills. Included were three historic pieces of legislation—the Taft-Hartley bill, the McCarran Internal Security bill, and the McCarran-Walter bill. (Congress did not challenge his vetoes of the offshore oil and independent gas producers bills.) Moreover, Congress also overrode one of his three vetoes of income-tax legislation. In the period from 1933 to 1981, Congress was not inclined to try to override a president on private or public bills with no significance for national policy-making, but it attempted to override the president

on about 3 of 5 regular vetoes of bills of national significance and was successful in overriding about 1 in 4.

The exercise of the president's regular veto power does
not end the battle between Congress and the White House
over the affected legislation. As indicated above, Congress
may override the veto, which has the effect of enacting the
bill into law, and the override may be considered a complete victory for the legislative body on that matter. Alter-
natively, Congress may persist by sending a similar bill
back to the president or his successor; if it is then signed
by the chief executive into law, the result may be considered a partial victory for Congress.

The president may also prevail in the battle. Congress's inability to act on a pocket veto or its failure to
override a regular veto may be considered a complete
victory for the chief executive. Moreover, the president or
a successor may sign into law a bill that is closer to his
view on the matter than to that of Congress.[18] This result
constitutes a partial victory for the president.

Finally, the battle may end in what is essentially a
compromise. This occurs when subsequent legislation is
passed that contains provisions favored by both the president and Congress, and it is not possible to say the view of
one prevailed over the other.

To determine the outcome of vetoes of nationally significant legislation, each of the affected bills was traced in
the same and subsequent sessions of Congress[19] through
the use of *Congressional Quarterly.* Because that journal
did not begin publication until 1945, the analysis begins with that year and ends in 1981. It therefore covers
seven administrations, beginning with that of President
Truman and ending with that of President Carter. Table
5.6 contains the essential information on the 199 vetoes of
nationally significant legislation cast during that period.

Table 5.6 indicates that a veto of a nationally signifi-

TABLE 5.6. Outcome of Presidential Vetoes of Nationally
Significant Legislation, 1945–1981, by President

|  | Victory for Pres. | | Victory for Cong. | | Compromise | | |
|---|---|---|---|---|---|---|---|
|  | No. | % | No. | % | No. | % | Total |
| Truman | 12 | 32.4 | 21 | 56.8 | 4 | 10.8 | 37 |
| Eisenhower | 14 | 41.2 | 9 | 26.5 | 11 | 32.3 | 34 |
| Kennedy | 1 | 25.0 | 1 | 25.0 | 2 | 50.0 | 4 |
| Johnson | 4 | 44.4 | 0 | 00.0 | 5 | 55.6 | 9 |
| Nixon | 5 | 13.2 | 12 | 31.6 | 21 | 55.2 | 38 |
| Ford | 18 | 32.7 | 20 | 36.4 | 17 | 30.9 | 55 |
| Carter | 10 | 45.5 | 4 | 18.2 | 8 | 36.3 | 22 |
| Total | 64 | 32.1 | 67 | 33.7 | 68 | 34.2 | 199 |

cant bill does not generally end the matter. The eventual
outcomes of conflicts between the president and Congress
from 1945 to 1981 were fairly evenly divided. The president won complete or partial victories on 64 bills, the
Congress on 67, and 68 battles ended in a compromise
that favored neither branch. Table 5.6 also shows that
Presidents Eisenhower, Johnson, and Carter tended to
win their battles with Congress over vetoed bills and that
Truman and Nixon tended to lose; Kennedy and Ford split
fairly evenly in their conflicts with the national legislature.

I also analyzed the outcomes of vetoes of nationally
significant legislation by general policy area. Because of
the "two presidencies" thesis, I expected to find that presidents would win more battles with the Congress on legislation relating to international involvement than they
would in the domestic areas of civil liberties and civil
rights, social welfare, and government management.
Table 5.7 shows that my hypothesis is confirmed. In legis-

lation relating to international involvement, presidents won victories over Congress by a 17–3 margin. In turn, the Congress prevailed over the president in the three domestic policy areas. At the same time, it should be noted that compromise between the two was fairly common in all policy areas with the exception of civil liberties and civil rights.

One final observation is in order with respect to the effect of the president's veto power on legislation. The veto should not be judged simply on the basis of how often it is actually exercised. By threatening to veto a proposed measure, the president can often deter Congress from passing it. A threat can also influence Congress to put a measure in a form that is acceptable to him. President Eisenhower successfully utilized the threat of a veto to affect social programs proposed by the Democratic Congress. This tactic worked because Democratic congressional leaders—Lyndon Johnson, majority leader of the Senate, and Sam Rayburn, speaker of the House—wished to avoid conflict with the popular chief executive and were willing to accept half a loaf rather than risk a presidential

TABLE 5.7. Outcome of Presidential Vetoes of Nationally Significant Legislation, 1945–1981, by General Policy Area

| Policy Area[a] | Victory for Pres. | | Victory for Cong. | | Compromise | | Total |
|---|---|---|---|---|---|---|---|
| | No. | % | No. | % | No. | % | |
| Civil liberties | 1 | 20.0 | 3 | 60.0 | 1 | 20.0 | 5 |
| International involvement | 17 | 58.6 | 3 | 10.3 | 9 | 31.1 | 29 |
| Social welfare | 18 | 24.3 | 25 | 33.8 | 31 | 41.9 | 74 |
| Government management | 28 | 31.8 | 36 | 40.9 | 24 | 27.3 | 88 |
| Total | 64 | 32.7 | 67 | 34.2 | 65 | 33.1 | 196 |

[a]It was not possible to classify three appropriation bills by policy area.

veto that they calculated could not be overridden. Spitzer's study of public veto threats beginning with those issued by President Kennedy indicates that although he and Johnson made no such public threats, Nixon utilized them on 5 occasions, Ford on 10, Carter on 12, and Reagan on 29 (1981 to 1986). His bar analysis shows that of those 56 total veto threats, in 13 instances the Congress backed down and the bill died; in 3 cases the president backed down and the bill was enacted; and 16 occasions resulted in a compromise. Twenty-four bills were passed as is and were vetoed; 5 of those vetoes were overridden. Most threats involved appropriation and spending bills. [20]

## NOTES

1. Max Farrand (ed.), *The Records of the Federal Convention of 1787* (New Haven: Yale University Press, l966), 2:74.

2. Ibid., p. 587.

3. Ibid., 4:81.

4. Jonathan Elliot, *The Debates in the Several State Conventions on the Adoption of the Federal Constitution* (Philadelphia: J. B. Lippincott Company, 1901), 4:621.

5. *The Federalist: A Commentary on the Constitution of the United States* (New York: Random House, 1937), No. 73, p. 477.

6. Ibid.

7. Joseph Kallenbach, *The American Chief Executive: The Presidency and the Governorship* (New York: Harper and Row, 1966), p. 354.

8. Edward Mason, *The Veto Power* (Boston: Ginn and Company, 1891), p. 139.

9. Ibid., p. 140.

10. Charles L. Black, Jr., "Some Thoughts on the Veto," *Law and Contemporary Problems* 40, no. 2 (Spring 1976):89.

11. Ibid.

12. Ibid., p. 92.

13. Louis Fisher, *Constitutional Conflicts Between Congress and the President* (Princeton: Princeton University Press, 1985), p. 143.

REASONS FOR AND EFFECTS OF VETOES

14. See Frank Prescott, "The Executive Veto in Southern States," *Journal of Politics* 10 (1948):659–675; M. Nelson Mc-Geary, "The Governor's Veto in Pennsylvania," *American Political Science Review* 41 (1947):941–946; Glen Negley, "The Executive Veto in Illinois," *American Political Science Review* 33 (1939): 1049–1057; and Roy Morey, "The Executive Veto in Arizona: Its Use and Limitations," *Western Political Quarterly* 19 (1966):504–515.

15. Roger Davidson, "The Presidency and Congress," in Michael Nelson (ed.), *The Presidency and the Political System* (Washington, D.C.: Congressional Quarterly Press, 1983), p. 374; Albert Ringelstein, "Presidential Vetoes: Motivation and Classification," *Congress and the Presidency* 12, no. 1 (Spring 1985): 43–55.

16. Particularly helpful in developing these reasons were the studies of gubernatorial vetoes listed in note 14.

17. R. Alton Lee, *Truman and Taft-Hartley: A Question of Mandate* (Lexington: University of Kentucky Press, 1966), p. 95.

18. In veto messages, presidents frequently indicate the specific provisions they object to in the legislation involved and may also suggest what they would like to see substituted. They may also express their views in press conferences and other public forums.

19. Bills were followed five years beyond the one in which the veto occurred under the assumption that if follow-up efforts on affected legislation were to be made, they would occur during that period of time.

20. Robert Spitzer, *The Presidential Veto: Touchstone of the American Presidency* (Albany: State University of New York Press, 1988), pp. 101–103. (He utilized the *New York Times Index* to get his information.)

# 6

# THE ITEM VETO

The item veto (sometimes referred to as the line item veto, although this term cannot be properly applied to the national level because congressional appropriations are not itemized by the line) has long been a matter of interest and controversy in American presidential and congressional politics. Related to this interest and controversy is confusion about what is included within the definition of an item veto.

The most common meaning of an item veto is the authority of a chief executive to *delete* one or more expenditure items in an appropriation bill while leaving the other items intact. A variant of that meaning is the power not only to delete an entire item or items but also to *reduce* it or them.

Another type of item veto allows a chief executive to delete *substantive provisions* of an appropriations bill. Such provisions can take various forms. One is a restriction, qualification, or condition on appropriations, such as stating that expenditures are not to be made for certain purposes or that they can only be made under certain conditions. In addition, other types of substantive provisions, often referred to as "riders,"[1] can be added to an appropriations bill: some riders may relate to the major purpose of the bill ("germane") and others may not ("nongermane").

Finally, there are other variations of the item veto.

One type is the *amendatory* veto, which grants the chief executive the power to conditionally approve a bill but to suggest changes in it. He or she may present amendments for the consideration of legislators. Another and most questionable form of the item veto (referred to as a *de facto* veto) is the legal power of the chief executive to interpret or to refuse to enforce certain provisions of bills passed by the legislature.

## THE ITEM VETO AT THE NATIONAL LEVEL

The item veto played no role in the early history of the nation. As indicated in Chapter 1, the regular veto was a matter of central concern at the Constitutional Convention, but the convention delegates did not even discuss the item veto. Moreover, the first president, George Washington, took the position that he had to approve or disapprove an entire bill and that he had no authority to veto a portion of it.

The first authority for an item veto appeared in the Provisional Constitution of the Confederacy, which provided that "the President may veto any appropriation or appropriations and approve any other appropriation or appropriations in the same bill." A similar authority was carried over into the Permanent Constitution of the Confederacy, which stated that "the President may approve any appropriation and disapprove any other appropriation in the same bill."[2] However, despite this authority, the president of the Confederacy, Jefferson Davis, never exercised the item veto.

The first president to explicitly request the power to exercise an item veto was Ulysses S. Grant (the request included the authority to reduce as well as to delete items in appropriations bills). His successors, Rutherford B. Hayes, Chester A. Arthur, and Grover Cleveland, also called for the power to exercise an item veto.

In the modern period, a number of presidents, Democrats and Republicans, liberals and conservatives, have asked Congress to grant them the power to exercise an item veto. Included are Franklin Roosevelt, Harry Truman, Dwight Eisenhower, Gerald Ford, Ronald Reagan, and George Bush. During the 1992 presidential campaign, Bill Clinton also called for an item veto.

The only president to come out specifically against the item veto was William Howard Taft. In his general treatise on the presidency, he stated his reservations about it as follows:

> While for some purposes, it would be useful for the Executive to have the power of partial veto, if we could be sure of its wise and conscientious exercise, I am not entirely sure it would be a safe provision. It would greatly enlarge the influence of the President, already large enough from patronage and party loyalty and other causes.[3]

Although one might anticipate that most presidents would favor an item veto that would add to their power, it might also be expected that members of Congress would be reluctant to grant such authority to the chief executive. However, in 1876, just three years after President Grant had asked for an item veto, Representative James Faulkner introduced a bill to grant the president an item veto. Over the years a number of similar proposals have been made. In 1986, it was estimated that they totaled 200.[4] However, despite such efforts, the only favorable floor action on such a bill occurred in 1938 when the

House of Representatives voted to give the president an item veto by statute.[5]

It would be a mistake, however, to conclude that the Congress is of one mind on the subject of an item veto. Its proponents have included such leading Democrats and Republicans, liberals and conservatives, as Arthur Vandenberg, Hubert Humphrey, Emanuel Celler, Kenneth Keating, Harry Byrd, Strom Thurmond, William Proxmire, Carl Curtis, Prescott Bush, Frank Carlson, Alben Barkley, Everett Dirksen,[6] Edward Kennedy, Joseph Biden, Alan Dixon, Robert Dole, Dan Evans, Jack Kemp, and Bill Bradley.[7] Its opponents have included Mark Hatfield, John Stennis, Lawton Chiles, Robert Byrd, Jr., Charles Mathias, James Wright, and Mickey Edwards.[8]

In addition to presidents and members of Congress, others have taken a position on the item veto. Favoring it have been such interest groups as the National Association of Manufacturers, the Chamber of Commerce of the United States, and the American Farm Bureau.[9] Opposing it have been Common Cause and the American Federation of Labor and Congress of Industrial Organizations.[10]

Public opinion polls taken by the Gallup organization in the post–World War II period indicate that most Americans favor an item veto. The approval rating in seven such polls conducted between 1945 and 1983 ranged from a low of 57 percent in 1945 to a high of 71 percent in 1978. (The ratings in 1981 and 1983 were 64 percent and 67 percent, respectively.)[11]

## THE ITEM VETO AT THE STATE LEVEL

Although the item veto in the Confederate Constitution was not adopted at the national level, it had an immediate impact upon the states. There were three categories of states. The first group consisted of the former states of the Confederacy that were required to formulate acceptable constitutions for readmission to the Union. The second group included new western states that were seeking admission into the Union. The third was older states that sought to modernize their original constitutions.[12]

The first state to adopt the item veto for its governor was Georgia in 1865. The next year, Texas did the same, followed by New York in 1867. (Iowa was the last to adopt it.)[13] Today the item veto exists in 43 states; the only ones that do not have an item veto are Indiana, Maine, Nevada, New Hampshire, Rhode Island, and Vermont and North Carolina, where the governor has no veto power at all. Moreover, no state that has adopted an item veto has ever repealed it.[14]

There are a number of reasons why states have adopted the item veto.[15] Initially the citizens were concerned with the venality of state legislators whom they trusted less than governors. Subsequently they progressively came under the influence of such ideas as "good government," "progressivism," the "executive budget," "consolidating gubernatorial powers," and fostering a "mature executive" at the expense of inefficient and parochial legislators.

There is considerable variety in the type of item veto devised in the states. Most common is the first type of veto described at the beginning of the chapter: the power of the governor to delete items from appropriation bills. However, in some cases, state chief executives are empowered to veto not only appropriation (dollar) amounts but substantive provisions as well. In ten states, governors may not only delete items but also reduce them. In most of these states, this gubernatorial power stems from explicit constitutional authority, but in Pennsylvania it is derived from court decisions.[16]

Another form of the gubernatorial item veto is the amendatory veto, which has been adopted in seven states. However, the provisions of these vetoes differ. For example, in South Dakota the governor may utilize the amendatory veto only to correct errors in the style or form of the legislation. However, in other states there is no limitation on the scope of the power and the veto can be used to make major policy changes in legislation. In Illinois, for example, the amendatory veto has had a profound impact on relations between the governor and legislators and has operated in favor of the former.[17]

The state that has gone the furthest with respect to the amendatory veto is Washington. The governor can use the "partial veto" not only on appropriation bills but on the monetary provisions in any bill. The partial veto can be utilized not only to improve the technical aspects of legislation but also to make substantive or policy changes.[18]

Many parties have sought state judicial decisions regarding gubernatorial item vetoes to clarify various interpretations of them.[19] One issue faced by the courts is what constitutes an "item" that is subject to the gubernatorial veto. For example, if the legislature places a condition on an appropriation, does that constitute an "item" that the governor can veto or is the veto restricted to the appropriation (dollar) amount itself?

An even more vexing problem for the state courts involves gubernatorial decisions to delete certain substantive provisions of a bill. The legal issue is whether the deleted provision is severable (so that the remaining bill is still logical and internally consistent and does not alter the basic intent of the legislature) or whether the deleted provision is not severable (that is, so intertwined with the remaining bill that the deletion defeats the purpose of the legislature). (Courts have tended to use the term "negative" to describe the first type of gubernatorial item veto and "affirmative" to characterize the second.)

A third area of state judicial conflict over the item veto involves the monetary scope of the power. Is the item veto power restricted to general appropriations or can it be applied to other types of monetary measures as well? In the latter category are special, earmarked revenue funds, as well as bond obligations. State courts have differed on this issue and the other two.

The complexities of these issues have led to a rapid increase in the number of state judicial decisions involving the gubernatorial item veto. It has been noted that from 1970 to 1984, there were about 50 decisions compared with 63 for the entire previous 77 years.[20] This development has led to judicial exasperation with the necessity of making difficult and highly subjective decisions involving gubernatorial item vetoes. A Florida court in a 1980 decision expressed its frustration: "It would be a serious mistake to interpret our jurisdiction in this case as a general willingness to thrust the Court into the political arena and referee on a biennial basis the assertions of power of the executive and legislative branches in relation to the appropriations act."[21]

There is little systematic comparative data on the amount of money that has been saved as a result of item vetoes cast by governors who possess the power. However, it was reported in 1984 that Governor James Thompson of Illinois cut 3 percent from appropriation bills,[22] Governor Ronald Reagan of California, 2 percent,[23] and Governor George Deukmejian of California, $1.2 billion.[24] On the other hand, the item veto is rarely utilized in Alabama because it has been the legislative practice there to appropriate money in lump sums.[25]

Some studies cast doubts on how effective the gubernatorial item veto is as an instrument of fiscal restraint. One study based on a 1982 mail survey of state legislative budget officers or chief staff members of the House appropriations committee (45 of 50 replied) concluded that "given its partisan use, the item veto has had a minimum effect in making legislatures in state government fiscally more restrained."[26] Another study involved an analysis of item vetoes cast in one state, Wisconsin, over the period from 1975 to 1985. This study determined that during that time, the highest annual savings as a result of item vetoes was 2.5 percent and the lowest annual savings was 0.006 percent. It also found that the vetoes were "not important as an instrument of fiscal restraint" but were "more important as a tool of policy-making or partisan politics."[27] Finally, another recent study of state per capita spending determined that spending in states in which the governor has no item veto power is no higher and may even be lower than in states with some form of item veto.[28]

## ALTERNATIVES TO A REGULAR
## PRESIDENTIAL ITEM VETO

Although unlike most governors, the president does not possess the item veto power, he can take actions that have a similar effect of negating portions of legislation he does not favor. One is to refuse to spend certain funds appropriated by Congress, an action referred to as *impoundment*. (It should be noted that historically this power gave a chief executive more authority than exercising an item veto because it was not subject to being over-ridden by Congress.)

## Impoundments

Impoundments have a long history in the United States.[29] After quarreling with members of Congress, President James Buchanan withheld funds from their districts. President Grant refused to spend money on projects of a "purely private or local interest." More recently, the practice of impounding funds gained momentum with the administration of Franklin Roosevelt. His impoundments and those exercised by Presidents Truman, Eisenhower, and Kennedy were directed primarily at military programs. In contrast, President Johnson concentrated his impoundments on domestic programs. However, he eventually changed course in the face of opposition of Congress and the states.

The practice of impounding funds changed radically during the Nixon administration. Nixon's impoundments were "of an entirely different order" and "set a precedent in terms of magnitude, severity and belligerence."[30] Congress reacted by passing the Impoundment Control Act of 1974. It provides for two types of impoundments: *deferral,* a temporary withholding of appropriations, and *rescission,* a permanent cancellation of appropriations. Both types require a special message from the president. A deferral can be disapproved by either house of Congress at any time: a rescission becomes inoperative unless it is approved by both houses within 45 days of continuous session.

In the 1980s the Supreme Court took actions that have had the effect of making presidential deferrals less certain. In a leading 1983 case, *Immigration and Natu-*

*ralization Service v. Chadha,*[31] the Court invalidated the one-house veto process on the grounds that it violated the principle of bicameralism and that Congress must act through both houses with respect to a bill presented to the president. Subsequently a federal circuit court ruled in *City of New Haven v. United States*[32] that the *Chadha* decision rendered the deferral action of the Impoundment Control Act of 1974 invalid because it was inseparable from the one-house legislative veto provision. However, the Court went on to explain that although the president could not utilize the deferral procedure for policy purposes, he could use it for programmatic or administrative ones. (The Congress promptly enacted that distinction into law.)[33]

Although the Impoundment Control Act of 1974 and subsequent court decisions have placed limitations on impoundments, they remain a potential weapon for presidents in reducing appropriations. This is especially true of rescissions. Fifty-nine percent of all rescission requests made by presidents from 1975 through 1984 were approved by Congress.[34] A broad analysis indicates that from the time of the enactment of the 1974 Impoundment Control Act through 1992, presidents sent Congress spending cut proposals totaling $69.3 billion and Congress enacted cuts—including many substitutions of its own—worth $71.0 billion.[35]

The situation in 1992 illustrates the kinds of political struggle that can develop between the president and Congress over rescission requests. President Bush's fiscal 1992 budget identified more than 4,000 spending projects to be killed that would have provided a virtually inexhaustible supply of rescission requests.[36] However, initially the president proposed 68 rescissions totaling $3.6 billion, most of which came from 1,398 potential cuts identified by the Office of Management and Budget.[37] Of the proposed savings, $3 billion was to come from the cancellation of the second and third Seawolf submarines, a project that the president had originally requested.

The president also sought to bring political pressure on the Congress. Among the rescissions he proposed were those related to the construction of local parking garages and to research on asparagus yields and prickly pears, projects he identified as "nothing but pork-barrel spending."[38] The president also vowed to work with the Republican membership of the House of Representatives to utilize a rule that allows only one-fifth of its members to move to discharge rescission bills from the House Appropriations Committee if it has not reported them within 25 days of continuous session. This move was designed to force the Democrats in the House to vote to reapprove or kill each of the individual projects that the president characterized as "pork-barrel spending."

The Democrats responded in kind. Leon Panetta of California, the chair of the House Budget Committee, said that the Democrats would have a rescission budget of their own. The concern was also expressed that the Republican plan to force a vote on scores of rescission proposals could require three or four hours of debate and voting time per project, thereby blocking the House from conducting any other business.[39]

Eventually, the Democrats prevailed in the 1992 rescission battle. President Bush expanded his rescission list to a total $7.9 billion. However, the Democrats' list exceeded his new list; their list totaled $8.2 billion. (The total projected deficit by the Office of Management and Budget for that year was $399.4 billion.) The major difference in the content of the two lists was the Democrats' decision to save one of the two Seawolf submarines but to insist on a cutback in the Strategic Defense Initiative and B-2 bombers. The Democrats also ridiculed "executive-branch pork," such as a study of sexual aggression in Nicaraguan fish and the mating behavior of swordfish. The Democrats in the House also controlled its procedure so that the Republicans had no meaningful chance to amend the rescissions or, in some instances, to even protest their plight. In one case, Democrats even ordered the TV cameras turned off in the House Rules Committee to deny angry Republicans the opportunity to make their case to a C-Span cable-TV audience.[40]

Also in 1992, two changes were proposed in the congressional procedure for considering presidential rescissions. One, referred to as "enhanced rescission," would alter the present procedure (rescissions do not go into effect unless *approved* by Congress within 45 days) to the opposite situation: Such rescissions would go into effect unless specifically *disapproved* by Congress. The other proposed change, referred to as "expedited rescission," occupies a middle ground between regular and enhanced rescission. The burden is the same as it is under current law in that presidential rescissions must be approved by Congress. However, unlike the present situation, under expedited rescission Congress cannot fail to act on rescissions: It must vote on them, even if the vote is one of disapproval.[41]

These proposals became important issues in late 1992. In his budget for the fiscal year 1993, President Bush called upon Congress to enact an enhanced rescission procedure. The House of Representatives instead passed, in early October, legislation introduced by Representative Tom Casper, Democrat of Delaware, that provided for a version of the expedited rescission procedure. The legislation amending the Impoundment Control Act of 1974[42] stipulated that the president would have three calendar days after signing an appropriation bill to submit to Congress a rescission message and an accompanying bill containing all proposed rescissions relating to the bill he signed. The president's bill would then be referred to the legislative branch in which the appropriation bill had originated; that body would have ten calendar days to act on it. If that branch agreed to the rescission bill, it would be referred to the other legislative branch where a similar procedure would be followed. Neither branch could amend the president's proposal, but some members of Congress interpreted the bill to allow the adoption of alternative rescissions. If a simple majority in either branch voted not to approve the president's rescissions, they would not go into effect. Finally, unless reenacted, the altered rescission procedure would be terminated when Congress adjourned in 1994. However, despite these restrictions and the fact that the measure passed the House by a 312 to 97 vote, the Senate failed to act on it.

Shortly after William Clinton was elected to the presidency, Speaker of the House Thomas Foley proposed that a procedure requiring Congress to act on presidential rescissions be substituted for an item veto that Clinton had previously endorsed. The president-elect said he would like to examine Foley's proposal. However, Senate majority Leader George Mitchell was guarded in his response to Foley's proposal, saying only that he was "less opposed at this time" to the Foley proposal than he was to an item veto.[43]

There is some disagreement over just how much would be saved if the president possessed an item veto as compared to the rescission power. An analysis by the General Accounting Office estimated that had such a veto existed, a savings of $70 billion could have been realized

over the six-year period 1984–1989.[44] However, Louis
Fisher of the Congressional Research Service estimates
that the actual savings would not have been $70 billion
but $2–$3 billion.[45] (After Fisher's testimony, the comptroller of the United States, Charles Bowsher, apologized
to Senate Appropriations Chairman Robert Byrd for the
General Accounting Office report, stating that the actual
savings could have been "close to zero" and that "one can
conceive of a situation in which the net effect of [line] item
veto power would be to increase spending.")[46] Finally, an
earlier report prepared for President Reagan by the Office
of Management and Budget went through appropriations
language for fiscal 1988 and deleted various programs; it
concluded that the item-veto authority might have saved
about $1 billion.[47]

*Signing Statements*

In addition to impounding funds appropriated by Congress, presidents have also attempted to exercise another
alternative to the regular item veto by making relevant
statements when they sign a bill. In the statements the
president may make various points. He may express the
intent not to enforce a provision of the bill on the grounds
that it is unconstitutional. He may state that it is against
the policy of the administration. Or the president may
give his interpretation of some provision of the statute.
The president may also justify his action on the grounds
that a particular provision of a statute was intended by
Congress to be only advisory rather than mandatory.

Like impoundments, the practice of signing statements has a long history.[48] Andrew Jackson signed a bill
and simultaneously sent to Congress a message that restricted its reach. President Tyler followed the custom by

signing a bill and then expressing misgivings about the constitutionality of the entire act. Woodrow Wilson signed a merchant marine bill but refused to carry out one section he found to be unconstitutional.

The issuance of signing statements has continued. When he signed the Military Authorization Act of 1971, President Nixon stated that one of its provisions (referred to as the Mansfield Amendment, urging the president to establish a final date for the withdrawal of all U.S. troops from Indochina) was against his judgment and the policy of his administration and had no binding force or effect. President Ford declared portions of a defense appropriations bill and a veterans' bill a "nullity" at the time he signed them, using the rationale that they constituted encroachments on executive powers.[49] President Carter decided to regard a statutory provision that the United States establish consular relations at a specified time and place as a recommendation rather than a mandate.[50]

The practice of signing statements persisted under Presidents Reagan and Bush. The former administration attempted to interpret the legislative intent of a bill the president was signing.[51] Also, in signing the Competition-in-Contracting Act of 1984, Reagan objected to a provision delegating certain duties to the comptroller of the United States as being unconstitutional.[52] President Bush also issued objections in signing statements of appropriations measures and in those relating to national security that he said were unconstitutional because they constituted improper legislative encroachments on his authority as head of the executive branch and as commander in chief.[53]

For the most part, the legality of signing statements has not been tested in the courts. However, in recent years, there have been some judicial warnings that signing statements may not be legal. A federal court in *LaCosta v. Nixon* called President Nixon's statement with respect to the Mansfield Amendment as "very unfortunate."[54] However, the court went on to point out that "executive initiatives taken before and since the law indicate no divergence from the national policy expressed in the Amendment." Similarly, in reviewing a case involving the Competition-in-Contracting Act of 1984, another federal court in *Ameron Inc. v. U.S. Corps of Engineers* stated that "this claim of the right of the President to declare statutes unconstitutional and to declare his refusal to execute them . . . is dubious at best."[55] However, the court also stated that "the question of the President's action, declarations, and purported refusal to order compliance with Competition-in-Contracting Act, however, are not properly before the Court." Another federal court in *Lear Siegler, Inc. Energy Products Division v. John Lehman, Secretary of the Navy* was much more emphatic in its rejection of President Reagan's action with respect to the Competition-in-Contracting Act.[56] It held that the president cannot bring a de facto line item veto into effect by promulgating orders to suspend parts of statutes that the president has signed into law, and that doing so would constitute an even more extensive power than that of an item veto because, unlike the latter, it would not be subject to being overridden by the Congress. The court went on to state that in declaring provisions of the act unconstitutional and suspending their operation, the executive branch assumed a role reserved for the judicial branch.

Two legal scholars[57] make the same points as those expressed in this judicial opinion, namely, that signing statements constitute an unconstitutional item veto that is not subject to being overridden by the Congress and that they inject the executive branch into the judicial process. They also argue that signing statements constitute "an unauthorized intrusion into Congress' lawmaking function," provide "a means of substituting presidentially-created policies for those of Congress," and are "unreliable, inaccurate, and misleading evidence of legislative intent." They go on to say that typical presidential signing statements merely note disapproval of a particular provision of a bill and express the president's desire that Congress make changes in the future. In contrast, "the new genre of such statements attempts to reinterpret the language of the bill so as to coincide with his own views."

## ARGUMENTS FOR AND AGAINST A PRESIDENTIAL ITEM VETO

The wide variety of arguments for and against the adoption of an item veto for the president can be grouped into three major categories.[58] The first is the success of gubernatorial item vetoes and their relevance for a presidential item veto. The second is the effect that a presidential veto would have on reducing federal expenditures. The third is the influence a presidential item veto would have on the constitutional balance among the branches of the national government.

### The Item Veto in the States

Those who favor an item veto for the president argue that it has worked successfully in states as demonstrated by the fact that no state that has adopted a gubernatorial item veto has ever withdrawn that authority. They also point to the above-noted comments by Governors Thompson of Illinois and Reagan and Deukmejian of California on how helpful the item veto was to them in their relations with their state legislatures. In addition, Representative Charles Bennett, Democrat of Florida, reported on the results of an informal poll of a larger number of governors showing savings accomplished by them through the use of the item veto.[59] The argument is also made that the threat of casting an item veto is an effective weapon in the hands of a state chief executive. Those who support a similar power for the president reason that such advantages would be transferable from the state to the national level.

Opponents of the presidential item veto tend to downplay the effectiveness of the state gubernatorial veto. They point to the fact that we have little in the way of comparative data on how the veto has actually operated in all 43 states that have the veto. In addition, they argue that the savings realized in the states that make the greatest claims about its use are relatively small, some 2 to 3 percent of appropriations. Moreover, as noted above, some studies determined that gubernatorial item vetoes acted more as a tool of partisan and policy politics than as an instrument of fiscal restraint.

Those who oppose a presidential item veto have a second line of defense as far as gubernatorial item vetoes are concerned: Even if one concedes that the vetoes have been effective, it does not follow that the state experience could be transferred to the national level because the situations differ so much.[60] State legislatures generally meet for shorter periods than the Congress does, making a gubernatorial item veto more necessary than a presidential one. Gubernatorial item vetoes are used in conjunction with balanced budget requirements in state constitutions but there is no such requirement at the national level. Many state constitutions require that appropriations bills be itemized (a procedure that facilitates the use of the gubernatorial item veto), but no such restriction applies to the Congress. Finally, governors exercise vetoes over geographical areas that are much smaller and more cohesive than that of the United States and are, therefore, more knowledgeable than the president about the validity of local projects.

## The Effect of a Presidential Item Veto on Federal Expenditures

Closely related to the state experience argument is the one relating to federal expenditures. Supporters of an item veto contend that members of Congress are notorious for logrolling, that is, voting for each other's pet projects as a means of currying the favor of their constituents and thereby getting reelected. The result is the inclusion in appropriation bills of pork-barrel legislation that benefits the districts of individual members of Congress but not the entire nation. The fact that such projects are lumped together in appropriation bills with those of merit places the president in the difficult situation of either vetoing an entire bill that includes good programs and projects or of signing a bill that contains pork-barrel projects. Contributing to the difficulty of the situation is the fact that Congress does not generally pass appropriation bills until the end of a legislative session so that there is little time to resolve matters. Granting the president the item veto power would enable him to eliminate pork-barrel projects from appropriations bills and to retain the sound ones.

Many argue against the contention that a presidential item veto would help reduce federal expenditures. Some say that Congress can and typically does appropriate in large lump-sum amounts, a practice preferred by both Congress and executive agencies because it accommodates the need for administrative discretion. Therefore, unless Congress substantially changes the structure of appropriation bills, the veto would give the president little control over individual projects or programs.[61]

Another argument relating to the effect of a presidential item veto on federal expenditures is that a relatively small proportion of such expenditures would actually be subject to a veto. Not covered would be such programs as Social Security, Medicare, Medicaid, welfare benefits, and retirement plans, all of which cannot be controlled without legislative changes in eligibility or benefit levels. Also outside the effect of a presidential item veto would be the interest on the national debt and measures for which Congress has made prior commitments. Also, it is unlikely that as commander in chief, most presidents would seek drastic cuts in national defense. The result is that only about 12 to 15 percent of the total federal budget would be subject to the item veto.[62]

Finally, opponents of a presidential item veto argue that it might increase rather than decrease federal spending.[63] If he possessed the item veto power, the president would be in a position to threaten a member of Congress that one of his pet projects would be deleted unless he agreed to vote for a program that the president favored, including one involving the expenditure of additional moneys. An item veto might also make members of Congress less fiscally responsible: They could include questionable projects in appropriation bills and if the president item vetoed them, tell their constituents that they did their best and were sorry that the president took action to negate them. Finally, it is argued that the historical record indicates that Congress has been more careful with public moneys than presidents have.[64]

*The Effect of a Presidential Item Veto
on the Constitutional Balance*

Differences also exist over the effect that an item veto would have on the relationships among the three branches of the national government. One scholar argues that the congressional practice of adding legislative riders and pork-barrel appropriations to vital bills forces the president to "throw out the baby to get rid of the bathwater."[65] The author suggests that since our nation's founding, the legislature has encroached on the president's veto power and that the "Founders would not find the item veto to be a dangerous innovation but rather a rehabilitation of an original and essential check and balance."[66]

Another student of the item veto expresses a diametrically opposed view on how the Founders would have regarded a presidential item veto. He argues that they would have thought that "the 'reform' brought about by an item veto would only accelerate the century-long trend toward executive dominance—nay supremacy—in its dealing with the legislature."[67] (He gives examples of that trend: the president's expanding war power, the use of executive agreements rather than treaties, the issuance of executive orders, the president's control over bill-drafting and the central clearance process and such budget-related powers as the formulation and establishment of budget practices, influence over the budget deliberation process in Congress, and the control over government spending by such devices as budgetary transfers, emergency spending, and secret spending.)

Another argument against an item veto is that it would be exercised not by the president himself but rather by career civil servants or unelected aides in the executive branch. A senior official in the Office of Management and Budget confessed, "Our ethos is presently that we are accountable to the President who looks out for the nation as a whole. But our perspective around here is rather narrow—we're concerned with our individual agencies, that's all, not the President's entire program." The official went on to state that the item veto is a "bummer" because it so fundamentally changes the relationship between the legislative and executive branches.[68]

Opponents of an item veto also contend that the experience at the state level demonstrates that federal courts would inevitably be forced to umpire disputes between legislative and executive officials. One close student of the subject suggests the following scenario.[69] "The president will first test the meaning of the item veto by reducing, not eliminating, appropriations. Second, the president will challenge the right of Congress to provide conditions under which an appropriation may be spent. Then the president will seek judicial approval for striking congressional conditions from appropriations. Finally, the president will seek to extend the coverage of the item veto to non-appropriations legislation." All these actions would probably have to be settled by the courts.

The result of an item veto would thus be most unfortunate. It would exacerbate conflicts between the legislative and executive branches. It would also force the judiciary to enter the fray despite the fact that it "is the branch least suited to mediate the budgetary process."[70] The consequence would be the shifting of action from the legislature to the executive, back to the legislature, and from both political branches to the courts. "As these items are bounced back and forth between the branches like a political shuttlecock, there will be substantial delays in the enactment of appropriations bills and uncertainty on the part of agencies, state government, and private citizens regarding their funding levels."[71]

## METHOD OF IMPLEMENTATION AND SCOPE
## OF A PRESIDENTIAL ITEM VETO

If one concludes that a presidential item veto is desirable, it is necessary to decide how the veto would be implemented. In addition, one needs to determine exactly what form the veto should take.

The approach that would require the least effort would be for the president to claim that he already possesses an item veto power and to proceed to exercise it. A New York attorney proposed that theory in 1987.[72] To substantiate his argument he pointed out that under the Constitution, the veto power applies to both "every bill" (Article I, Section 7, Paragraph 2) and to "every order, resolution or vote" (Article I, Section 7, Paragraph 3). The president could therefore determine that a "bill" contained implicit "joint resolutions" for each item or rider and then veto selected resolutions within a bill at his discretion. He further suggested that whatever result the courts might ultimately reach on the issue, the use of the power offers the president everything to gain and nothing to lose because the courts can deliver no worse than the status quo.

Others support the theory of an implied item veto power. George Will, a columnist for the *Washington Post,* cited the fact that in May 1991, four senators and 44 representatives urged President Bush to assert his implied item veto power. He also suggested that the Supreme Court might side with the president and even if it sided with the Congress, it would focus attention on

"Congress' defense of indefensible practices." Or the Court might declare the matter a "political issue," in which case a "serious" president would prevail in the battle of the two branches in the court of public opinion.[73] An editorial in the *Wall Street Journal* also urged President Bush to assert his item veto power, which would force Congress to "defend its pork in public." It went on to suggest that the matter would go to the courts and even if they sided with Congress, that would leave matters no worse than they are now.[74]

Others, however, have been very skeptical about the validity of an implied item veto power for the president. This group includes members of recent presidential administrations as well as legal scholars;[75] Charles Cooper, an assistant attorney general in the Justice Department's Office of Legal Counsel in the Reagan administration, said that the idea of such a power cannot be supported by constitutional theory. James C. Miller III, budget director under President Reagan, also expressed the opinion that their group had been unable to find a constitutional power to justify the exercise of an implied item veto. Even constitutional scholar Robert Bork, speaking to a group of conservatives, called the idea of an implied item veto "dubious" and apologized for having "to be the one to rain on your parade." Moreover, Louis Fisher, a specialist in congressional and executive relations at the Congressional Research Service of the Library of Congress, said that if the president tried to item veto particular legislation and the case were taken to the Supreme Court, the vote against the president would be 9–0. Finally, it should be noted that neither President Reagan nor President Bush followed the urging of some conservatives that they unilaterally exercise an item veto. In fact, on March 20, 1992, in an address to Republican members of Congress and presidential appointees, President Bush said that his attorney general and White House counsel, backed by legal opinions from most legal scholars, felt that the president does not presently have the item veto authority. He went on to note that this view was shared by the attorney general in the Reagan administration.[76]

A less sweeping assertion of an implied item veto power is the contention that the president has the authority to negate a nongermane rider that is unrelated to the rest of a bill. C. Boyden Gray, White House counsel in the Bush administration, said in 1991 that he would not rule out the possibility that the president would someday exercise that power, which he referred to as a "so-called subject veto."[77] Scholars are divided on the matter. One close student of the subject argues that "support for construing a bill to embrace for purposes of the presidential veto, an interconnected piece of legislation dealing with related subject matter may be found in the rules of both Houses of Congress prohibiting nongermane amendments."[78] Another counters with the argument that "the power to veto individual sections of a piece of legislation is more than the power to reject, for it is the power to alter legislation. A piece of legislation is a product of a complex interaction between individual legislators, interest groups, the public, and the President himself."[79]

Those who favor an item veto for the president but feel he does not presently possess one have proposed a variety of methods for implementing it. These proposals differ in substance, and some will be more difficult to adopt than others.

The method that would require the least change from the present situation was proposed by President Franklin Roosevelt. He suggested that "the legislative branch of the Government can pass legislation with the item veto in it. The whole process could, it seems to me, be tested out by inserting a simple clause in the appropriation bill and applying it only to that bill. This at least would get the matter before the Senate, and I think I am right in saying that an amendment of this kind to an appropriation bill could be brought up on the Floor at the time the bill was pending."[80]

Other related proposals also call for congressional action but encompass all appropriation bills rather than individual ones as suggested by President Roosevelt. One is a statutory declaration that each item or provision in an appropriation bill is to be considered a separate bill for purposes of the veto section of the Constitution.[81] Another proposal by Senator Mark Mattingly, Republican of Georgia, is to direct the secretary of the Senate and clerk of the House to split appropriation bills into parts and to send each part to the president as if it were an individual bill subject to veto.[82] Still a third approach advocated by Harry Byrd, former Democrat from Virginia, would be to amend the rules of the Senate and the House, so that appropriation bills had to contain a provision authorizing the president to disapprove any item in them.[83]

Another general approach to implementing an item veto would be to have Congress grant the president the authority by statute. Senator Mattingly introduced such a bill with the grant of authority confined to a two-year trial experiment.[84] Other proposals would give the president a de facto item veto through changes in rescission procedures. One sponsored by Senator William Armstrong, Republican of Colorado, and Senator Russell Long, Democrat of Louisiana, would have established quarterly targets for growth in the ceiling on the amount of outstanding federal debt. If targets would otherwise be exceeded, the president could then reduce spending by up to 20 percent.[85] Another proposal along the lines of the enhanced rescission introduced by Senator John McCain, Republican of Arizona, and Daniel Coats, Republican of Indiana, would have altered the rescission procedure by giving the president the right to cancel spending unless both the House and Senate voted to reject the rescission. (It will be recalled that under the present law, presidential rescissions are not effective unless both houses of Congress vote to approve the rescission within 45 days of continuous session.) The president could then veto that rejection, forcing Congress to attempt an override by a two-thirds majority in both houses.[86]

The statutory approach to an item veto is much easier to accomplish than one involving a constitutional amendment. (During Reagan's first term, for example, an amendment that would have facilitated new anti-abortion laws, an equal rights amendment, and another that would have allowed organized, spoken prayer in the public schools all went down to defeat.)[87] However, there is some question of the legality of a statutory item veto. Some authorities point out that some state courts have found the statutory veto to be unconstitutional.[88] Moreover, the Congressional Research Service suggests two reasons a statutory item veto may not be constitutional. One is that the Constitution sets out a very detailed description of the legislative process and provides a limited legislative role for the president, one that cannot be enlarged without violating the Constitution. The other is that to "so enlarge the role of the president in the process of enacting legislation is to create a 'potential for disruption' of the legislative process."[89]

Over the years, most advocates of an item veto have proposed a constitutional amendment to accomplish that purpose. Senator Arthur Vandenberg, Republican of

Michigan, introduced such amendments during both the Roosevelt and Truman administrations.[90] Senator Byrd offered a similar amendment during the Eisenhower administration.[91] Senator Mattingly (in addition to the statute noted above granting the president an item veto) introduced a constitutional amendment to accomplish that same result. Other similar resolutions were introduced by Representative Jack Kemp, Republican of New York, and Representative Henry Hyde, Republican of Illinois.[92]

As indicated above, over the years numerous proposals have been made for a constitutional amendment to grant the president an item veto. However, not one has been adopted. Suggestions have been offered to make such a proposal acceptable to members of Congress. One is to have the constitutional amendment provide for conferring the authority by subsequent legislation (which could be repealed by Congress by the passage of another statute) rather than confer the authority directly by the amendment itself.[93] Another is to allow presidential item vetoes to be overridden by Congress by a simple majority vote.[94] (There is some question, however, whether such a provision is legal since the Constitution spells out explicitly that a two-thirds vote in both houses is necessary to override a presidential veto.)

In addition to determining how authority for an item veto should be implemented, there is the issue of what specifically should be included within that authority. In the early years of the Eisenhower administration, the Legislative Reference Division of the Bureau of the Budget recommended that an item veto include the power to disapprove any item appropriating money; to disapprove any textual provision in any appropriation bill that could appropriately be the subject of a separate bill, including both legislative riders on appropriation items and general legislative provisions; and to reduce any item appropriating money when the president chooses to do so in preference to eliminating the whole item.[95] Later in that same administration the Bureau of the Budget suggested that an item veto apply to authorization bills as well as appropriation ones.[96] Senator Vandenberg had also proposed in the Roosevelt administration that such a veto extend to tax bills.[97]

In early 1993 Senator Bill Bradley, Democrat of New Jersey, introduced a bill to grant the incoming president an item veto over both appropriation and tax bills. He proposed that in order to avoid constitutional obstacles, each item in every appropriation and tax bill be enrolled as a separate bill after it had been passed by Congress. The president could then sign the entire bill or single out individual items to sign or veto. The bill also provided that it remain in effect for only two years. The senator suggested that this sunset provision would allow the courts to address possible constitutional issues that might arise and would also permit the Congress and the White House to thoroughly evaluate the consequences of the procedure.[98]

## NOTES

1. Jack Plano and Milton Greenberg, *The American Political Dictionary,* 7th ed. (New York: Holt, Rinehart, and Winston, 1985), p. 226. They suggest that the term "rider" applies to a provision that is unlikely to pass on its own merits and that is added to an important bill so that it will "ride" through the legislative process.

2. Russell Ross and Fred Schwengel, "An Item Veto for the President?" *Presidential Studies Quarterly* 12 (Winter 1982):66.

3. William H. Taft, *Our Magistrate and His Powers* (New York: Columbia University Press, 1916), pp. 27–28.

4. Louis Fisher and Neal Devins, "How Successfully Can the States' Item Veto be Transferred to the President?" *Georgetown Law Journal* 75, no. 1 (October 1986):185.

5. Ibid., p. 159, n. 4, citing 83 Cong. Rec. 355–56 (1938).

6. Ross and Schwengel, "An Item Veto," p. 73.

7. Thomas Cronin and Jeffrey Weill, "An Item Veto for the American President?" (Paper delivered at the 1985 Annual Meeting of the American Political Science Association, New Orleans, La., August 29–31), app. C.

8. Ibid.

9. Ross and Schwengel, "An Item Veto," p. 73.

10. Cronin and Weill, "An Item Veto," app. C.

11. Thomas Cronin and Jeffrey Weill, "An Item Veto for the President?" *Congress and the Presidency* 2, no. 2 (Autumn 1985):136.

12. Ronald Moe, "Prospects for an Item Veto at the Federal Level: Lessons from the States" (Paper delivered at the 1985 Annual Meeting of the American Political Science Association, New Orleans, La., August 29–31), p. 7.

13. Louis Fisher, "The Item Veto: The Risks of Emulating the States" (Paper delivered at the 1985 Annual Meeting of the American Political Science Association, New Orleans, La., August 29–31), p. 2.

14. Alan Dixon, "The Case for the Line-Item Veto," *Notre Dame Journal of Law, Ethics, and Public Policy* 1, no. 2 (1985):211.

15. Moe, "Prospects," pp. 10–28.

16.Fisher and Devins, "How Successfully," p. 166, citing *Commonwealth v. Barnett,* 199 Pa. 161, 48 A. 976 (1901).

17. Moe, "Prospects," p. 9, citing John Walters, "The Illinois Amendatory Veto," *John Marshall Journal of Practice and Procedure* 11 (Winter 1977/78):416. Moe at p. 29 also noted that 33 states have a procedure that enables the legislature to recall a bill from the governor's desk before it is signed. This enables the chief executive to determine what provision or provisions should be altered before he signs it; this action amounts to a de facto amendatory veto.

18. Ibid., p. 10.

19. Two excellent analyses of such decisions are Fisher and Devins, "How Successfully," pp. 168–178; and Moe, "Prospects," pp. 31–38.

20. Fisher and Devins, "How Successfully," pp. 177f.

21. Ibid., p. 177, citing *Brown v. Firestone,* 382 So 2d 654 (Fla. 1980), 671.

22. Alan Dixon, "The Case for the Line-Item Veto," p. 213, citing Palffy, *Line Item Veto: Trimming the Pork,* 343 Heritage Foundation Backgrounder (1984), p. 8.

23. Ibid.

24. Ibid.

25. Moe, "Prospects," p. 40.

26. Glenn Abney and Thomas Lauth, "The Line-Item Veto in the States: An Instrument for Fiscal Restraint or an Instrument for Partisanship?" *Public Administration Review* 45, no. 3 (May-June, 1985):377.

27. James Gosling, "Wisconsin Item Veto Lessons," *Public Administration Review* 46, no. 4 (July-August 1986):297.

28. Moe, "Prospects," p. 39, citing Benjamin Zycher, "Institutional and Mechanical Control of Federal Spending," in "Control of Federal Spending," C. Lowell Harris (ed.), *Proceedings of the Academy of Political Science* 35, no. 4 (1985):142.

29. Louis Fisher, *Constitutional Conflicts between Congress and the President,* 3d ed. rev. (Lawrence: University Press of Kansas, 1991), p. 129.

30. Ibid., p. 196.

31. 462 U.S. 1919 (1983).

32. 809 F. 2d 900 (D.C. Cir. 1987).

33. Fisher, *Constitutional Conflicts,* p. 130, citing 101 Stat. 785, sec. 206 (1987).

34. Robert Spitzer, *The Presidential Veto: Touchstone of the American Presidency,* (Albany: State University of New York Press, 1988), p. 139, citing Louis Fisher, *The Constitution between Friends* (New York: St. Martin's Press, 1978), p. 182; and Palffy, *Line Item Veto,* p. 2.

35. H. Rept. No. 103–44, 103d Cong., 1st sess. (1993), p. 30.

36. *Congressional Quarterly Weekly Report,* March 21, 1992, p. 713.

37. Ibid., March 28, 1991, p. 792.

38. Ibid., March 21, 1992, p. 713.

CHAPTER SIX

39. Ibid.
40. Ibid., May 9, 1992, p. 1238.
41. For an analysis of these rescission proposals, along with the item veto power, see the statement of Louis Fisher of the Congressional Research Service before the House Committee on Rules, 102d Cong., 2d sess., September 25, 1992.
42. The provisions, debate, and vote on HR 2164 appear in the 1992 Congressional Record—House, 10805-10816 and 10975, 10976.
43. *Washington Post,* November 16, 1992.
44. Report to congressional committees by the General Accounting Office (January 1992).
45. 138 Cong. Rec. 55882 (daily edition, April 39, 1992).
46. *Congress Daily,* September 18, 1992, p. 3.
47. Report to the President from James C. Miller, Director of the Office of Management and Budget, March 10, 1988.
48. Fisher, *Constitutional Conflicts* , pp. 128, 130.
49. Spitzer, *The Presidential Veto,* p. 139, citing Fisher, *The Constitution between Friends,* p. 93.
50. Ibid., citing Louis Fisher, *The Politics of Shared Power* (Washington, D.C.: Congressional Quarterly Press, 1981), p. 25.
51. Ibid.
52. Fisher, *Constitutional Conflicts,* p. 130.
53. *Congressional Quarterly Almanac* 46 (Washington, D.C.: Congressional Quarterly, Inc., 1990), p. 16.
54. 55 R.F.D. 145 (E.D.N.Y. 1972), 146.
55. 987 F.2d 875 (3d Cir. 1986), 889.
56. 842 F.2d 1102 (9th Cir. 1988), 1124, 1125.
57. Marc Garber and Kurt Wimmer, "Presidential Signing Statements as Interpretations of Legislative Intent: An Executive Aggrandizement of Power," *Harvard Journal on Legislation* 24, no. 1 (Winter 1987):363–395.
58. Ross and Schwengel, "An Item Veto," p. 74.
59. Dixon, "The Case for the Line-Item Veto," p. 213, citing "Item Veto." Hearings before a Subcommittee of the House Judiciary Committee, 83d Cong., 2d sess. (1954), p. 4.
60. Fisher, *Constitutional Conflicts,* pp. 132f.
61. Fisher and Devins, "How Successfully," p. 186.
62. *Proposals for Line-Item Veto Authority* (Washington,

184

D.C.: American Enterprise Institute for Public Policy Research, 1984), p. 16, citing a *Washington Post* article.

63. Cronin and Weill, "An Item Veto," in *Congress and the Presidency,* pp. 140f.

64. Spitzer, *The Presidential Veto,* p. 133, citing Norman Ornstein, "Veto the Line Item Veto," *Fortune,* January 7, 1985, pp. 109–111.

65. Judith Best, "The Item Veto: Would the Founders Approve?" *Presidential Studies Quarterly* 14, no. 2 (Spring 1984):187.

66. Ibid., p. 185.

67. Robert Spitzer, "The Item Veto Reconsidered," *Presidential Studies Quarterly* 15, no. 3 (Summer 1985):612.

68. Cronin and Weill, "An Item Veto," in *Congress and the Presidency,* pp. 139f., citing a personal interview with an unidentified OMB official.

69. Moe, "Prospects" pp. 51f.

70. Fisher and Devins, "How Successfully," p. 195.

71. Ibid., p. 197.

72. Stephen Glaser, *Wall Street Journal,* December 4, 1987.

73. *Washington Post,* February 23, 1992.

74. *Wall Street Journal,* February 26, 1992.

75. *Congressional Quarterly Weekly Report,* May 14, 1988, pp. 1284f.

76. *Public Papers of the Presidents,* 1992, at p. 512.

77. *National Journal,* May 18, 1991, p. 1193.

78. Richard Givens, "The Validity of a Separate Veto of Nongermane Riders to Legislation," *Temple Law Quarterly* 39 (1965–66):63.

79. Richard Riggs, "Separation of Powers: Congressional Riders and the Veto Power," *University of Michigan Journal of Law Reform* 6, no. 3 (Spring 1973):756.

80. Letter dated March 9, 1942, from President Roosevelt to Senator Arthur Vandenberg, OF 47, Veto Message Abstracts, 1942–1945, Franklin D. Roosevelt Library.

81. Memorandum dated February 14, 1953, "The item veto on appropriation bills" from Roger Jones, Assistant Director for Legislative Reference, Bureau of the Budget, to B. M. Shanley, p. 6, OF 99-J, Vetoes, Box 356, Dwight D. Eisenhower Library.

82. Dixon, "The Case for the Line-Item Veto," p. 225, citing

S.J. Res. 178, 98th Cong., 1st sess., 129 Cong. Rec. 13, 591–92 (1983).

83. Letter dated March 12, 1953, from Senator Harry Byrd to President Eisenhower, OF 99-J, Vetoes, Box 356, Dwight D. Eisenhower Library.

84. *Congressional Quarterly Almanac* 40 (Washington, D.C.: Congressional Quarterly, Inc., 1984), p. 153.

85. Dixon, "The Case for the Line-Item Veto," p. 224, citing proposed amendment No. 2625 to S. 2062, 98th Cong., 1st sess., 129 Cong. Rec. S16318 (1983).

86. *Congressional Quarterly Weekly Report,* February 29, 1992, p. 459.

87. *Congressional Quarterly Weekly Report,* January 21, 1984, p. 115.

88. Memorandum dated February 14, 1953, from Roger Jones to B. M. Shanley, p. 6, OF 99-J, Vetoes, Box 356, Dwight D. Eisenhower Library.

89. Dixon, "The Case for the Line-Item Veto," p. 225, citing S.J. Res. 178, 98th Cong., 1st sess., 129 Cong. Rec. 13, 591–92 (1983).

90. In a letter dated August 19, 1937, Senator Vandenberg wrote to President Roosevelt seeking his support for an item veto and referred to the fact that the senator had presented a constitutional amendment to accomplish that result in the last and present sessions of Congress. OF 47, Veto Messages, 1936–1939, Franklin D. Roosevelt Library. Another letter dated September 24, 1945, from the senator to President Truman referred to another constitutional amendment proposal that was before the Senate Judiciary Committee. OF 47, Harry S Truman Library.

91. Letter dated March 12, 1953, from Senator Byrd to President Eisenhower, OF 99-J, Vetoes, Box 356, Dwight D. Eisenhower Library.

92. *Congressional Quarterly Weekly Report,* January 21, 1984, p. 115.

93. Letter dated January 30, 1959, to Representative Richard Poff, Republican of Pennsylvania, from Maurice Stans, Director of the Bureau of the Budget, OF 99-J, Vetoes, Box 356, Dwight D. Eisenhower Library.

94. Dixon, "The Case for the Line-Item Veto," p. 222, citing
S.J. Res. 26, 98th Cong., 1st sess., 129 Cong. Rec. S836-38 (1983).
95. Memorandum dated February 14, 1953, from Roger
Jones to B. M. Shanley, OF 99-J, Vetoes, Box 356, Dwight D.
Eisenhower Library.
96. Letter dated January 30, 1959, to Representative Richard Poff from Maurice Stans, OF 99-J, Vetoes, Box 356, Dwight
D. Eisenhower Library.
97. Letter dated August 19, 1937, to President Roosevelt
from Senator Vandenberg, OF 47, Veto Messages, 1936–1939,
Franklin D. Roosevelt Library.
98. *Congressional Quarterly Weekly Report,* January 16,
1993, p. 123; *Wall Street Journal,* January 13, 1993.

# 7

## CONCLUSIONS

The Founders made a wise choice in deciding on a qualified veto and vesting it in the president alone rather than requiring him to share it with members of the judiciary. The fact that only about one-quarter of regular presidential vetoes in recent years have been overridden by Congress indicates that it is a potent weapon without being an absolute one. It would be unwise for judges to have a part in vetoing legislation that they might have to later rule upon. Moreover, the practice of judicial review means that judges do possess a type of ultimate veto in passing upon the constitutionality of legislation enacted by Congress.

The evolution of the veto power also indicates that it is sufficiently broad so that individual presidents can utilize it for purposes that they think are important and proper. At the same time, analysis of vetoes in the modern era shows that presidents tend to exercise vetoes in certain circumstances, namely, when they are having difficulty getting Congress to enact legislation they request or favor, during presidential and congressional election years, and when the nation is experiencing significant inflation or unemployment. This means that the veto power is available for use when the president differs with the Congress on important political and policy matters.

James Wilson's rationale for the veto power—that as a "man of the people," the president has the "fullest information" about the nation's situation, including access to foreign and domestic records and communications as well as advice from executive officers in the different departments of the general government—has proved to be an excellent one. Over the years of this study, the advice given by the various executive departments has become increasingly systematized and coordinated. The Legislative Reference Division has become the central clearance agency, gathering information and recommendations from the various agencies concerned with legislation; it uses this information and these recommendations to advise the president on whether to exercise the veto.

At the same time, presidents have developed other sources of advice on enrolled legislation. These include members of the White House staff, cabinet officials, and persons inside and outside the government. A practice has also developed of creating special policy positions within both the White House and the Office of Management and Budget to provide advice on veto decisions; the two types of officials often meet directly with each other, cutting the Legislative Reference Division out of the process. Increasingly, the director of the Office of Management and Budget also gives his personal advice to the president on enrolled legislation, which often varies from that of the Legislative Reference Division within his agency. Presidents also have created special White House units to elicit views of members of Congress and interest groups. (Persons serving in these units are also used to help carry out presidential decisions on vetoes.)

However, not all advice on enrolled legislation originates as a result of presidential requests. A number of persons and groups outside the executive branch attempt to influence veto decisions, particularly members of Congress. Also involved have been state and local officials, political party and campaign officials, interest group representatives, and members of the public. This broad array of sources gives chief executives the "fullest information" that Wilson feels is a major rationale for the president's veto power. The Legislative Reference Division provides a programmatic and substantive view of enrolled legislation, which serves to help protect the institutional presidency. Advice that comes from a variety of other persons within the executive and legislative branches furnishes a political and policy perspective designed to guard the personal interests of the president. Communications from persons outside the national government help to ensure that the president is, as Wilson suggested, a "man of the people" as far as veto decisions are concerned. These diverse sources and perspectives serve to sensitize presidents to a variety of considerations involved in decisions regarding presidential vetoes.

Analysis of veto messages developed during the advisory process indicates that presidents follow the suggestions of Madison and Hamilton and also find other reasons for vetoing legislation. These include not only the constitutional and legislative encroachment ones specified by these two Founders but also those involving fiscal unsoundness, administrative unworkability, and bad public policy. The fact that the particular focus of this last, most prevalent reason is that certain legislation favors a specific group parallels closely Madison and Hamilton's concern about "factions" harming the public good. This broad rationale for exercising the president's veto power makes that power effective.

An analysis of the public-policy effects of the president's veto power also indicates that the veto is a potent weapon. As previously indicated, most vetoes are not overridden by Congress. If new legislation dealing with the general subject of a vetoed bill is introduced in Congress, there is a good chance that it will end in the enactment of legislation that is closer to the president's preferred version or in a compromise between the two branches of government. In addition, the president can use the threat of a veto not only to defeat the legislation but also to put it in a form acceptable to him. This means that the president's veto power can be used not only to negate legislation but, as Madison argued, to "revise" it as well.

Because the presidential veto as originally devised, and as it has worked out in practice, is basically a sound principle, major changes, including the presidential item veto, are not needed. The claim that the item veto would result in substantial savings is simply not borne out by the evidence. The proportion of the federal budget to which it would apply is relatively small; moreover, recent analyses indicate that projected reductions in expenditures that would have resulted through the use of an item veto were minimal. For the most part, the funding levels of presidential budgetary requests and congressional appropriations are very similar, with the latter sometimes being lower than the former. The real fiscal difference between the two branches lies in their respective *policy* priorities.

The proposal to grant the president an item veto authority ignores the fact that the president already possesses a range of powers that he can use to affect federal spending. The budget, in which the president presents his spending priorities to Congress, is the starting point for the discussion of fiscal matters. When this budget goes before congressional committees, members of the president's administration can defend his budget and try to influence committee and floor decisions on it. The president can also take his case to the American people, asking them to put pressure on their representatives and senators to uphold the president's position. If all else fails and Congress passes appropriation items the president does not favor, he can use his regular veto power on the entire bill and ask the Congress to pass a new one he favors; he can also use his rescission authority. The proof of the cumulative effect this array of powers has on federal expenditures is that Congress goes along with an overwhelming proportion of presidential budgetary requests.

Rather than serving as an instrument of fiscal restraint, the item veto would much more likely become a political weapon in the hands of the president. He might be expected to use it against projects and programs favored by political opponents, including not only members of Congress from the opposite political party but also those of the president's own political party who differ from him on important policy matters. The president probably would use the item veto against projects in small states with few electoral votes (an exception is New Hampshire because of its importance in presidential nominations) and approve those in large states with many electoral votes. Finally, the president could use the item veto power to bargain with members of Congress, threatening to use it against their favorite projects unless they vote for his programs or nominees to cabinet or judicial positions.

Instituting an item veto would damage the relationship between Congress and the president and tip the existing balance of power in favor of the executive. Extending the veto to cover tax bills, as Senator Bradley has proposed, would save more money than the current veto power, which applies only to appropriation bills, but such an extension would further exacerbate the relationship between the two branches of government. Allowing these major elements of public policy to be determined by the president and one-third plus one members of one house of

Congress present and voting on the issue (vetoes must be overridden by a two-thirds vote in both houses) would be particularly objectionable because the power of the purse is the oldest prerogative of legislative bodies.

Although the deficit has created a favorable political climate for an item veto, it will be difficult to implement one. There is little, if any, legal justification for the president's acting on his own to exercise such a veto. Nor is it likely that Congress will change its procedures to separate individual items in appropriation and/or tax bills so that the president can veto them, or that the legislators will grant the chief executive the item veto power by statute, especially since that raises constitutional issues. Finally, it is questionable whether Congress will, by a two-thirds vote of both houses, be willing to initiate a constitutional amendment to vest an item veto power in the president. The facts that none of these actions has been taken to date by Congress—and that current congressional leaders such as Senate Majority Leader George Mitchell and Senate Appropriations Committee Chairman Robert Byrd oppose an item veto—indicate that serious obstacles exist in the adoption of such a power.

My own view is that an expedited rescission procedure along the lines of the one voted on favorably by the House of Representatives in October 1992 would be a much better reform than the item veto. Even though the president's rescission requests could be negated by either house of Congress by a simple majority vote, rather than the two-thirds vote in both houses required to override an item veto, the expedited procedure would have other advantages for a president. Congress does not itemize appropriation bills, which means that the president cannot get at a bill's individual items, but after appropriation bills are enacted into law, he can go inside appropriation accounts and make them the subject of rescissions. Under an expedited procedure, the Congress would be required to vote for or against presidential rescissions rather than nullify them by taking no action as is permissible under current law. Also, Congress is more likely to grant the president an expedited rescission power than an item veto one; Speaker Foley has endorsed expedited rescission, and, as indicated above, the House of Representatives has overwhelmingly voted in favor of it. (It remains to be seen whether Senate leaders and members will be as amenable to the reform.) Finally, an expedited procedure can be accomplished by statute whereas an item veto would probably require a constitutional amendment.

Despite the advantages of an expedited rescission procedure for the president, it would also contain protections for the Congress. Although that body could not amend the president's rescissions, it would or should be able to adopt alternative rescissions. If either house voted against approval of presidential rescissions, they would not go into effect. Moreover, the expedited rescission procedure would be terminated in two years unless Congress reenacted it. Thus, expedited rescission is a viable alternative to an item veto. It is a compromise solution that protects the legitimate interests of both the president and Congress. At the same time, it has a reasonable prospect of adoption.

Two legal matters pertaining to the president's veto power remain unresolved. The first concerns the circumstances under which a president can use a pocket veto; the second is the legal effect of a signing statement. It will be recalled from Chapter 1 that in recent years Congress and the executive branch have taken diametrically opposed positions on the pocket veto issue. The former argues that if Congress appoints agents to receive bills during intra- or intersession adjournments or recesses, the president must use a regular veto that Congress can override. Congress believes that a pocket veto applies only to the end of an entire two-year Congress. In turn, the executive branch contends that the pocket veto may be used anytime Congress adjourns or recesses for more than three days; it derives this argument from the language of Article 1, Section 5 of the Constitution, which requires either house to obtain the consent of the other before it adjourns for more than three days.

The Supreme Court should resolve this first issue. My own view is that the congressional position is the correct one. As long as agents are appointed by Congress to receive bills during an adjournment or recess, it is difficult to see how their return has been "prevented" as stipulated in Article 1, Section 7. Moreover, Congress is not required to act within a certain time on bills received when it is in session. The position of the executive branch that the pocket veto procedure should operate when Congress adjourns for more than three days is indefensible because it means Congress is almost forced to remain in virtually continuous session or face the prospect of what amounts to an absolute veto. Tying the pocket veto procedure to the requirement that either house must obtain the consent of the other if it adjourns for more than three days is to argue in favor of a false analogy.

The Supreme Court should also decide the issue of presidential signing statements. My opinion is that they should have no legal effect. The president should not have the right to nullify a section of a statute simply because it does not support the policy of his administration. He should not have the power to substitute his policy preferences for those of an equal branch of the government, Congress. The contention that the president can refuse to enforce a provision of a statute on the grounds that it is unconstitutional is incorrect: It is the province of the courts, not the chief executive, to make that determination. The argument that the president can interpret the meaning of a provision of a statute is unconvincing. That decision should be the function of Congress unless that body specifically delegates the decision to the president; if there is any doubt, the matter should be resolved by the courts. Also, a statement by the president that he considers a certain provision of a statute as being only advisory and not mandatory on Congress' part is presumptuous and should not be permitted unless the legislative body clearly indicates that such is the case. The president should be able to express his objections to certain provisions of a bill in a signing statement, but those objections should have no legal effect. Their purpose should be confined to trying to convince Congress to make changes in the legislation in the future or to informing the public about the president's views on the matter.

Despite these two remaining issues, which need to be resolved, the veto power in general has operated well both in terms of public policy and in terms of relations between Congress and the president. In my view, it would be unwise to alter it by adopting an item veto.

# INDEX

# INDEX

# INDEX

# INDEX

# INDEX

# INDEX

# INDEX

# INDEX

Presidential box score, 44, 45–46(table), 47
Presidential Commission on Subversion and Civil Liberties, 112
Presidential power, 173, 192
Presidential support score, 44, 45–46(table), 47, 52, 54
President's personal background, 40–43, 51
Price control bills, 76
Private legislation, 32, 33–34, 35
  vetoes, 36
Protestant churches, 14, 21
Proxmire, William, 156
Public influence, 105, 121–126
Public interest, 143, 144(table)
Public lands, 76
Public legislation, 32–33, 35, 55, 61(n1)
  significant, 35, 36–39, 45–46(table), 49(table), 54, 55–61, 145–149
  vetoes, 35–36, 39, 41, 42(table), 45–46(table), 49–50(tables), 54–55, 56, 59, 60, 147–149
Public Liaison Aide, 88
Public opinion polls, 47–48, 49(table)
  on item veto, 156
Public works, 58

Rafshoon, Gerald, 88
Railroad retirement bill, 108–109
Randolph, Edmund, 11–12
Rayburn, Sam, 106, 107, 111, 114, 149
Reagan, Ronald, 179

and item veto, 155, 159, 166, 170, 176
  pocket veto, 23, 24
  signing statement, 167, 168
  veto threat, 150
Reconstruction program, 17
Reed-Bullwinkle bill, 114
Regulations, 40
Reorganization Plan 1 (1939), 72
Reorganization Plan 2 (1970), 81
Republican presidents, 40, 41, 42(table), 56, 59(table), 60, 61, 118, 140, 141
Republicans, 43, 59–60, 82, 85, 108, 163, 164
Rescission, 178, 193, 194
  expedited, 195
  *See also under* Impoundment
Research on Aging Act (1972), 82
Retirement plans, 172
Revenue legislation, 55
  vetoed, 56
  *See also* Tax bills
Revolution of 1643 (England), 5
Rhode Island, 6, 157
Rhodes, John, 108
Ringelstein, Albert, 138
Ripley, Randall, 57
Robertson, David, 123
Robinson, Joe, 122
Rockefeller, Nelson, 84
Rohde, David, 39, 49
Roman Empire, 1, 2–4, 5–6, 7
Rommel, Wilfred S., 80, 81, 84
Roosevelt, Franklin D., 31
  impoundments, 161
  and item veto, 155, 177–178
  veto and congressional

# INDEX